Gospel Coach
Workbook

Scott Thomas

Cover Design by Jeff Lopez Designs

Jefflopezdesigns.com

DEDICATION

This workbook is dedicated to Pastor's Kids (PK's) everywhere. I had two of the best PK's who are not perfect, but are loved wholly by their grateful parents. My prayer is that a new generation of PK's will grow up in healthy homes as they, as a family, serve King Jesus.

CONTENTS

C2C NETWORK

The C2C Network is a uniquely Canadian network that exists as a catalyst for church planting and church multiplication. Psalm 72:8 inspired the name, "May He have dominion from sea to sea and from the River to the ends of the earth." C2C works with church planters, existing churches, denominations, and networks across Canada with three guiding values: Gospel-Centered, Spirit-Led, and Mission-Focused. More information may be found on the website, www.c2cnetwork.ca

ENDORSEMENTS

Gospel Coach is the coaching system that C2C Network utilizes to develop our church planters. It perfectly complements our guiding principles of being gospel-centered, Spirit-led, and mission-focused.

- Gord Fleming, National Director, C2C Network

The flock needs shepherds who will be committed to knowing, feeding, leading and protecting the sheep. I am excited to see how Gospel Coach has been used by the Lord to train pastors, church planters, and leaders to care for His people. This workbook is an important tool to develop more and more competent shepherds and healthy churches.

- Timothy Witmer, Professor of Practical Theology Westminster Theological Seminary and author of *The Shephera Leader* and *The Shephera Leader at Home*

I've seen my friend Scott Thomas shepherd church leaders for years. Scott is aware of the issues leaders face in their personal, spiritual, and ministry lives. Gospel Coach is a practical and theologically rich book that will help produce healthy leaders to lead missional churches.

- Ed Stetzer, President of LifeWay Resources

Gospel Coach takes the mystery out of coaching by sharing how women in ministry can have an intentional coaching relationship. Our female voice is needed for the advancement of the mission of the church , and Gospel Coach gives an easy to use tool for coaching others to follow in our footsteps.

- Shari Thomas, Founder and Director of Parakaleo, co-author of *Beyond Duct Tape: Holding the Heart Together in a Life of Ministry*

HOW TO USE THIS WORKBOOK

The Gospel Coach Workbook supplements the material in *Gospel Coach: Shepherding Leaders to Glorify God*. This Workbook is designed to be utilized in the Gospel Coach Certification Training. *Gospel Coach*, published by Zondervan remains the primary resource to gain a full understanding of how to Gospel Coach. Instead of repeating any information, beyond a few quotes and illustrations, this workbook represents fresh material that is based on the foundations of Gospel Coach, but not in a repetitive manner.

For those participating in the training, it would be beneficial to have the workbook in hand and interact with the material as it is presented. The questions are designed to be discussed in groups of three or four people. Space is made available to write answers within the book.

The Gospel Coaching Workbook will walk step by step through the material, outlining the major points to consider as you learn to be a Gospel Coach that shepherds others toward the Chief Shepherd, Jesus.

It would be helpful for participants if they read Chapter 1 prior to the training. This gives the background for the creation of Gospel Coach.

1 WHO'S SHEPHERDING YOU?

A well-known Christian leader took me to a quirky coffee shop in Seattle—one of hundreds such shops in the Pacific Northwest—and he startled me with a question that ignited the Spirit's work in my life. That single question resulted in the creation of Gospel Coach. I was handling some serious issues that had arisen in the mega-church where I served as a Pastor and Executive Elder. The man sitting across the table was the President of another church planting network. He had experienced his own series of ministry issues, and had a winsome concern for others. While sipping on our coffee, he asked me about the gravity of the church problems and then leaned in, folded his hands, and in a whispered tone asked me a life-changing question: "Who's shepherding your soul?"

I answered this well-respected leader with a seemingly mocking echo. I tend to resort to humor (or at least my version of it) when I am embarrassed at my shortcomings. I similarly folded my hands, leaned in, and whispered, "Nobody."

The truth was that I was in community with several other pastors. I had a business coach, a supervisor, and a board of directors, and fellow employees surrounded me every day. But none of those relationships could be described as "shepherding of my soul."

Frankly, I didn't see the point. We didn't have time for shepherding. We had churches to start, leaders to develop, theological positions to consider. I surely recognized that shepherding might have some value, but it was not treasured to me. That is, not until a church planter in our network killed himself.

Pastor Ty (not his real name) was a friend of mine. The news that he yelled at his wife for two hours in their bedroom, and then pulled the trigger on a handgun aimed at his own head, shocked me. Ty and I made plans to go to Scotland the next summer and play golf on the old courses. Interestingly, he told me that was on his "bucket list."

Ty was a "successful" church planter. His church baptized eight people the Sunday prior to his suicide, and they had their highest attendance in three years of existence. His wife later told me that they had been experiencing marital problems for years. I had multiple dinners with them, and I didn't suspect anything that would lead me to believe they were struggling. But then, I didn't ask either.

I assumed because he was experiencing a vibrant ministry that his marriage and family and soul were vibrant, as well. I was horribly wrong. I asked myself how I could consider myself a friend and not even ask about other areas of his life.

Shepherding is Leading

In the midst of this untimely death, I remembered what the Christian leader said to me in the coffee shop, "Who's shepherding your soul?" I wondered what that meant. I asked a team to research everything they could find on shepherding. They surveyed Scripture, books, websites, periodicals, and ways in which other Christian organizations shepherded their leaders. After reflecting on the research, I discovered that shepherding is leading. In fact, "Biblical church leadership and gospel coaching are, at heart, shepherding."[1] See *Gospel Coach*, chapter 6 for further explanation.

I still didn't know what to do with this profoundly evident fact. I read and re-read the 76 pages of notes on shepherding. I reflected on my quarter of a century of Christian ministry. I had led youth ministries, churches as a lead pastor, and directed an International church planting network. But I had not shepherded in the compelling way that was described in Scripture. I let this conviction and the words of Scripture soak into my heart.

Suicide Round Two

I got a call from an elder that they had terminated the employment of their founding pastor. The elder and I talked about transition and for caring for their ex-pastor. The church had about 500 people in attendance after five years. This was a significant church plant in our network.

The next evening, a text informed me that this recently fired pastor was in the hospital with kidney and liver failure. It was troubling news that came just four months after Pastor Ty committed suicide. Blake (not his real name) suffered from insomnia and had an addiction to sleeping pills. He started taking Tylenol PM to get off the prescription medication. The night that he was let go, he took too many doses and died. Speculation still exists whether it was an accidental overdose. The state medical examiner, however, declared it a suicide.

I attended the second funeral of a deceased church planter in four months. It was two too many. I didn't want to do that ever again.

Now What?

A week later, I walked into an event with fellow members of our organization where I was leading a coach training. I had a heavy heart over the tragic loss of these two pastors. I had just finished talking with one of our board members on the phone discussing these tragedies and how to communicate it honestly, but respectfully with the Christian community.

I told the 15 church planters/coaches in training gathered, that I felt we needed to "shepherd" our growing number of church planters as well as coach them, but that we could not ask the busy planters to schedule a coaching call, and an additional shepherding call. I asked if anyone had any ideas. All that I got was blank stares. How were we going to build a system of caring for the personal, relational, and spiritual needs of church planters while we coached them in their church plants?

> How were we going to build a system of caring for the personal, relational, and spiritual needs of church planters while we coached them in their church plants?

Research confirms that coaching (sometimes called mentoring) is attributable to productive church planting, measured by external factors. We didn't want to cease coaching, but we could not ignore the other needs.

While someone in the group was leading a portion of the coaching training, I sensed the Spirit impressing on my heart, "It's shepherd-coaching." When that person was done talking, I paused the training sequence and asked them what they thought about incorporating shepherding into coaching. The all responded favorably, like I had just offered to buy their steak dinner that night. It was the initial confirmation that this was a Spirit-led idea.

Acts 20:28 came to my mind in that moment and it was a guide to the new shepherd-coaching concept. The Apostle Paul gathered the Ephesian elders and warned them:

> *Pay careful attention to yourselves and to all the flock of God, in which the Holy Spirit has made you overseers, to care for the church of God, which he obtained with his own blood.*

Throughout the workbook, answer the questions to the best of your ability. The answers are commonly found in the endnotes.

What is the main idea in Acts 20:28?[2]

_____

_____

_____

_____

_____

Why is it necessary to care for the church of God?[3]

_____

_____

_____

_____

_____

In what two ways does this passage suggest that a leader accomplish this?[4]

_____

_____

_____

_____

_____

> If a leader does not pay careful attention to their selves, that leader is essentially disqualified to pay careful attention to the flock

Theologian John Calvin pointed out in his commentary on Acts 20:28 that if a leader does not pay careful attention to their selves, that leader is essentially disqualified to pay careful attention to the flock.[5] Unhealthy leaders produce unhealthy disciples and unhealthy organizations. The Holy Spirit has entrusted the lives of certain people to the oversight of church leaders. Leaders must equip the saints (mend, repair, make whole) for the work of the ministry to build up in maturity and grow up the church in ALL aspects into Christ (Ephesians 4:11-16).

The table below shows these two complementary aspects of caring for the church:

Pay Careful Attention to **Self**	Pay Careful Attention to **Flock**
Being	*Doing*
Who we are	*What we do*

Who we **are** precedes what we **do**. This is opposite what our culture values. We ask one another, "What do you **do?**" Consequently, what we do wrongly dictates whom we perceive our selves to be. This creates all kinds of issues as we will discover throughout our training.

Gospel Coaching is mending, building, and growing up disciples to emulate Christ in every area of their lives. Expositor's Greek Testament described it this way:

> This means more than that we are to grow into resemblance to Him, or that our growth is to be according to His example. It means that as He is the source from which the grace or power comes that makes it possible for us to grow, He is also the object and goal to which our growth in its every stage must look and is to be directed.[6]

The source, means, and aim of our coaching is Christ and the goals of our coaching are informed by the gospel.

2 GOSPEL COACH GOALS

The term *coach* originally referred to a horse-drawn carriage for the purpose of transporting people and mail. This horse-drawn carriage (depicted above) was originally manufactured in the small Hungarian town of Kocs, in the fifteenth century. Kocs is pronounced in English, "coach." Coaching, in its original intent, refers to the process of transporting an individual from one place to another.[7] It is not necessary to make it more complicates than that.

Gospel Coach has five clear goals:
1. Develop a reproducible and natural system to make disciples
2. Practical process to develop and equip leaders in the local church.
3. Shepherd leaders to lead effectively; shepherd the shepherds.
4. Provide a gospel-centered foundation for coaching
5. Minimize bad decisions.

1. Develop a Reproducible and Natural System to Make Disciples

Gospel Coach is primarily a disciple-making system. The mission of almost every church is to make disciples as mandated in the Great Commission: "Go therefore and make disciples of all nations, baptizing them in the name of the Father and of the Son and of the Holy Spirit, teaching them to observe all that I have commanded you" (Matt. 28:18-20). The problem exists that we do not know what we are making. Write your definition below:

In your own words, what is a disciple?

_____
_____
_____
_____
_____

> While most coaching systems focus primarily on skills, Gospel Coach combines three mentor relationships into one:
> 1. **Discipler** - Basic skills to know and obey Jesus
> 2. **Spiritual Guide** - Accountability, decisions and direction
> 3. **Coach** - Skill Development
>
> *Connecting: The Mentoring Relationships You Need to Succeed* by Paul Stanley and Robert Clinton.

Jesus Made Disciples

It appears that Jesus developed disciples through what could be described as a classic coaching system. In Luke 9:1-6, Jesus sent the Twelve Apostles to preach the gospel. Read Acts 9:1-6 and 9:10 and consider the following question:

What did they do in Luke 9:10 and how is this a coaching or mentoring relationship?

_____
_____
_____
_____
_____

In Luke 10:1-16, Jesus sent 72 disciples in groups of two to pray for laborers and to engage the community to proclaim the Kingdom.

How did Jesus "coach" them after sending the 72 disciples (Luke 10:17-24)?[8]

_____
_____
_____
_____
_____

2. Practical Process to Develop and Equip Leaders in the Local Church

The Apostle Paul's disciple, Timothy, was an example of developing and equipping leaders through coaching skills.

What are some elements of coaching found in the relationship between Paul and Timothy (2 Timothy 1:1-7)?[9]

_____
_____
_____
_____
_____
_____
_____
_____

3. Shepherd the Leaders to Lead Effectively; Shepherd the Shepherds

Paul sent Titus to the Island of Crete and commissioned him to establish the elders in each of the churches. Titus was not a seasoned leader when Paul first met him. In fact, Titus was a convert of Paul. Coaching is a means to shepherd leaders to lead effectively in a healthy manner.

1. Titus was a friend who encouraged Paul (2 Corinthians 7:6).
2. Titus faithfully accomplished ministry responsibilities for Paul (2 Corinthians 8:6; 12:17).
3. Titus developed a heart for the ministry (2 Corinthians 8:16-17).
4. Titus became a proven minister (2 Corinthians 8:23).
5. Titus was the senior overseer who appointed elders in Crete (Titus 1:4-5).

The local church is now taking responsibility for the training and development of church leaders. How could coaching accelerate that process?[10]

_____

_____

_____

_____

_____

4. Provide a Gospel-Centered Foundation for Coaching

The gospel is both the motivation and the means for coaching. Some coaching is pragmatically-driven. This is where the coach seeks to solve problems without considering any antithesis to the principles of the gospel. For instance, a person may ask his coach to help him to consider how to increase his income. The pragmatic coach may ask questions about the possible sources of income and will perhaps ask about possible cuts in expenses. However, a gospel coach would address the motivation behind the need for increased income. The gospel coach seeks to uncover idols beneath the needs.

We cannot address our problems with humanistic, man-centered solutions. "Carl Rogers's 1951 book *Client-Centered Therapy* defines counseling and therapy as a relationship in which the client is assumed to have the ability to change and grow by a therapeutic alliance formed between the clinician and client."[11] This included unconditional blanket acceptance of the client's choices. Rogerian therapeutic methods can be summarized by the following:[12]

1. **Self-Actualization**, the full realization of one's potential originally developed by Abraham Maslow and his Hierarchy of Needs.
2. **Client-Centered Therapy**, where the focus is on the needs of the client, regardless of priority.
3. **Non-directive** describes the therapists role as a reflector and responder, and never an initiator or corrector.
4. **Mankind is inherently good**, the humanistic belief that people will discover the answers to their problems if asked the right questions.

Gospel-centered coaching, on the other hand, deliberately addresses the issues of sin, rebellion, forgiveness, redemption, and restoration. The Gospel Coach directs or instructs the disciple when necessary, with listening skills and interactive conversations.

5. Minimize Bad Decisions

Victory is won through many counselors (Proverbs 11:14). Trusted and experienced advisers are needed to help us make wise decisions. Proverbs 15:22 tells us, "Plans fail for lack of counsel, but with many advisers they succeed." A Gospel Coach advises the disciple to assist their making good decisions and minimizing bad decisions. Coaching is not the silver bullet to avoid bad decisions, but it is a bullet. It avoids decision-making in a vacuum.

Gospel Coach Commitment

Gospel coaches make the following commitment to their disciples.

1. I commit to glorify God by shepherding disciples in a holistic manner with the Gospel.
2. I commit to make the Gospel of Jesus Christ the primary focus of every coaching session.
3. I commit to shepherd disciples' hearts for Gospel transformation.
4. I commit to hold to the authority and sufficiency of Scripture.
5. I commit to equip disciples to exhibit Gospel implications as image-bearers of God.
6. I commit to promote the local church as the seat of ministry where community, mission and the Gospel exude to the world.
7. I commit to coach church leaders to be qualified, gospel-empowered developers of other church leaders producing healthy, disciple-making churches.

Gospel Coach Training

Foundation	Competencies	Tools	Practicum
1. Goals of Coaching 2. Gospel Centrality 3. Basics of Coaching	4. Coach Qualities 5. Shepherd Skills 6. Conversation	7. C.R.O.S.S. 8. Pre-session questions	9. Coach Practice 10. Two Disciples + Ten Sessions
Equipped to	competently coach	disciples in the	power of the gospel

What three questions do you hope are answered in the Gospel Coach Training?

1. _____

2. _____

3. _____

What things need to be developed in your life to coach others effectively?

_____

_____

3 GOSPEL-CENTERED COACHING

Gospel Coach is committed to make the Gospel of Jesus Christ the primary focus of every coaching session (see full list above). This sounds good in theory, but what does it look like practically?

It Starts with an Understanding of the Gospel

Coaching can be done *without* the gospel. It can even be helpful to a point. Coaching that addresses the behavioral changes needed to have a life more productive than one without changes is beneficial. For instance, if one were coached how to put together a resume or CV in order to find a job, that would be helpful. The missing element that the gospel would include is discerning the motivation for seeking a new job, including finding identity in status or material things, redeeming broken relationships, and being truthful. So, almost all coaching can be helpful. It is not my intent to disrespect other coaching systems. Gospel Coach has a differing focus, but it does not make it essentially *better*.

The difference is that Gospel Coach commits to shepherd disciples' hearts for gospel transformation, rather than behavioral modification, to produce positive outcomes. The glory of God is the primary goal, not self-actualization. Redemption is the focus, not remedies to the problems of a person. Gospel Coaching is not client centered; it is gospel-centered. Rather than being non-directive, it is gospel-directed. It does not start with a belief that people are basically good with all the answers within them; it starts with a belief that God is good and has given us His Helper, the Spirit of truth to lead people into all truth (John 16:13; 14:15-17).

Tim Chester wrote in his helpful book, *Closing the Window: Steps to Living Porn Free,* "Where my heart leads, my behavior follows."[13] We can help people to overcome their debilitating behaviors through counsel and white-knuckle determination, or we can lead them to the gospel where real heart change occurs. Our desires must first change before our behavior changes.

Coaching with the Gospel

Without the Gospel	With the Gospel
Behavioral Modification	Gospel Transformed Lives
Self-Actualization	Glory of God is the Focus
Remedy for Problems	Redemption through Christ
Client-Centered	Gospel-Centered
Non-Directive	Gospel Directed
Humans are Good	God is Good

How can our coaching reflect the gospel (1 John 5:3-5, 11-13)?

_____

_____

_____

_____

_____

"In fact, this is love for God: to keep his commands. And his commands are not burdensome, for everyone born of God overcomes the world. This is the victory that has overcome the world, even our faith. Who is it that overcomes the world? Only the one who believes that Jesus is the Son of God... And this is the testimony: God has given us eternal life, and this life is in his Son. Whoever has the Son has life; whoever does not have the Son of God does not have life. I write these things to you who believe in the name of the Son of God so that you may know that you have eternal life" (1 John 5:3-5, 11-13, NIV).

The Gospel Story

Augustine said that the Gospel of John is deep enough for an elephant to swim and shallow enough for a child not to drown. The same is true of the gospel of Jesus Christ. The gospel is hard to define. It is better described as a story than a definition. The gospel is "God's good news about the cradle, the cross, and the crown," as J. I. Packer describes it. The summary of the gospel story is described in four narrative acts of creation, fall, redemption, and restoration. This is God's story about mankind's redemption through His Son Jesus Christ.

Gospel's Four Acts	Implications
1. Creation • God • Creation • Harmony	Worship, community, love of others, stewardship of earth
2. Fall • Disobedience • Consequence • Need	Trust broken, idols, selfish, fearful, abuse of good gifts
3. Redemption • Promise Made • Promise Kept	Jesus is the worship, community, love, and approval for which we deeply long.
4. Restoration • All things New • Forever with God	Repentance

Coaching Centered on the Gospel

Scriptures teach that the problems we have are inside the heart and mind.

> "For from within, out of the heart of man, come evil thoughts, sexual immorality, theft, murder, adultery, coveting, wickedness, deceit, sensuality, envy, slander, pride, foolishness." (Mark 7:21-22)

> "The heart is deceitful and desperately sick; who can understand it?" (Jeremiah 17:9)

All sin is unbelief in the Gospel. Disciples with unbelief in the Gospel are believing someone or something else is the source of their identity, happiness, and fulfillment. For instance, we may think our role as a parent is the source of our identity. If that drastically changes, we lose our identity, value, and worth. David Powlison said, "The motivation question is the lordship question. Who or what 'rules' my behavior, the Lord or a substitute?"[14] The gospel is the ultimate solution for every problem we face, and the answer is obviously not something we find within the gospel.

Our Coaching Must be Centered on the Gospel

Forgiven sinners are made right through Jesus Christ alone.
"for all have sinned and fall short of the Glory of God...as it is written: 'None is righteous, no, not one'" (Romans 3:10, 23).

"Repent, then, and turn to God, so that your sins may be wiped out, that times of refreshing may come from the Lord" (Acts 3:19, NIV).

The problems we have exist inside the heart and mind and the solution is Christ.

And you were dead in the trespasses and sins in which you once walked, following the course of this world, following the prince of the power of the air, the spirit that is now at work in the sons of disobedience— among whom we all once lived in the passions of our flesh, carrying out the desires of the body and the mind, and were by nature children of wrath, like the rest of mankind. (Eph. 2:1-3)

> # In Gospel Coach, we don't have to feel the pressure to give good advice...we are freed to give Good News!

Our coaching must recognize that disciples will sin, and make bad decisions, break promises, and fail miserably at times. The gospel provides a solution through the forgiveness of Christ (1 John 1:9). The disciple does not have to hide things from or pretend with the coach. Instead, the more sin is confessed and acknowledged, the better it will be for the disciple to walk in obedience. The coaching rhythm is what is called a Three-Step Gospel Waltz.

Three-Step Gospel Waltz

In a waltz, the dancers have three steps that are repeated over and over (as if I would have a clue). It sounds redundant and tedious, but when done properly, the waltz is a beautiful thing to observe. In coaching with the gospel, the disciple recognizes their need of the gospel, often through the pain of circumstances. The coach leads the disciple to repent, to exercise faith that leads to belief, and to live in obedience to God's commands. Just as in the dance, the three-step gospel waltz will need to be repeated in close relationship with a coach: 1-2-3, 1-2-3, repent, believe, obey, repent, believe, obey. A coach encouragingly helps a disciple to do this repetitively.

Three-Step Gospel Waltz

Repent	Believe	Obey
The time is fulfilled, and the kingdom of God is at hand; repent and believe in the gospel (Mark 1:15)	For by grace you have been saved through faith. And this is not your own doing; it is the gift of God, not a result of works, so that no one may boast (Eph. 2:8-9).	For godly grief produces a repentance that leads to salvation without regret, whereas worldly grief produces death (2 Cor. 7:10).
I need rescued by Christ.	I am righteous through Christ's righteousness and have full forgiveness, even in the midst of my sin (2 Cor. 5:21).	Because I am a forgiven child of God whom God is well-pleased, I desire to obey my Father's will.

The law corrects us, but the grace of God changes us. By His grace, we have access to God through the death, burial, and resurrection of Christ.

Look over the table on the next page. What position in Christ is the most meaningful to you and why?

_____

_____

_____

_____

_____

Our Position in Christ

1. Dead to sin (Rom. 6:11)	11. Free from the Law (Rom. 8:2)
2. Spiritually Alive (Rom. 6:11)	12. Crucified w/Christ (Gal. 2:20)
3. Forgiven (Col. 2:13)	13. Light in the World (Mt. 5:14)
4. Declared Righteous (1 Cor. 1:30)	14. Victorious over Satan (Luke 10:19)
5. A Child of God (Rom. 8:16)	15. Cleansed from Sin (1 Jn. 1:7)
6. God's Possession (Titus 2:14)	16. Declared Blameless (Phil. 2:15)
7. Heir of God (Rom. 8:17)	17. Set Free from the desires of flesh (Gal. 5:24)
8. Blessed with all Spiritual Blessing (Eph. 1:3)	18. Secure in Christ (1 Pet. 1:3-5)
9. Citizen of Heaven (Phil. 3:20)	19. Granted Peace (Rom. 5:1)
10. Set free from power of sin (Col. 2:11-15)	20. Loved by God (1 John 4:10)

Leading with the Gospel

The graphic below shows an alternate way of leading. Rather than being rooted in abilities, experience, and education, the gospel-centered leader is rooted in their identity and position in Christ (see table above).

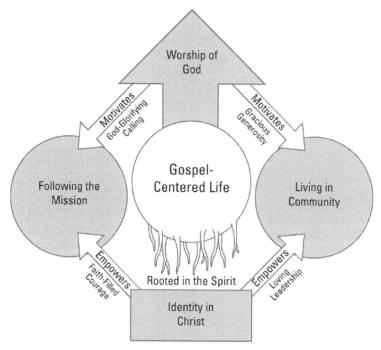

Because of the gospel, we are declared the beloved children of God, in whom the Father is well pleased. His Spirit affirms this within us. This frees us to worship God, rather than our selfish success. This vertical alignment is necessary before pursuing mission and community.

Too many young leaders focus on mission and community—a horizontal relationship—without nurturing a relationship rooted in the gospel—a vertical relationship.

What are the challenges to coaching with Gospel-centrality?

_____
_____
_____
_____
_____

Distortions of Gospel-Centered Leadership

The outcomes of a life rooted in identities of Christ, available through the gospel, and a worshipful spirit of the completed work and rescue of Christ, is that mission would increase and community would be established.

What four attributes motivate and empower mission and community?[15]

_____
_____
_____
_____
_____

Mission and community grow _out of_ a life centered properly in the gospel. Jesus said, "Follow me and I will make you fishers of men" (Matthew 4:19). As we follow Christ, He changes our life and it always leads to His mission and His people. Drew Dyck, managing editor of Leadership Journal wrote in his forthcoming book, _Yawning at Tigers_:

> "When we get a vision of who God truly is, suddenly we're energized to do his mission. Once we gaze on his grandeur and glory, obedience becomes easy. It's not a duty—it's a joy. We want to live for him. Our voices join Isaiah's willing reply, 'Here I am! Send me.'"[16]

It is common for leaders to begin focusing on the outcomes of this vision of God and to lose sight of God. It happened to me. At first I wanted to serve Him out of a heart of trust and gratitude. Later, I served the mission out of duty with a hat tip to God. We absolutely believe the gospel, but lose the steadying centrality of the vertical relationship with God through the gospel. As the illustration below depicts, mission and community are birthed, motivated, nurtured, and developed out of the gospel.

The problem is not a focus on mission and community, but an obsession with mission and community—quietly superseding our relationship with God.

More   **More**

How could this be a problem, after all, I thought we were supposed to advance His Kingdom?[17]

_____

_____

_____

_____

_____

Jesus retreated often to spend time with His Father in prayer. Before He began His public ministry, Jesus fasted forty days and forty nights in the wilderness. Jesus was sent to "seek and to save the lost" (Luke 19:10), but His customary manner was to pray. Consider the words of Luke 22:39-41:

> And he came out and went, **as was his custom**, to the Mount of Olives, and the disciples followed him. And when he came to the place, he said to them, "Pray that you may not enter into temptation." And he withdrew from them about a stone's throw, and knelt down and prayed (emphasis added).

Before we pursue mission and community, we must be captured wholly by God. The gospel provides our identity, which rests securely in Christ and the gospel provides access to God, the focal point of our lives.

This is like a pendulum from which the weight of the gospel swings back and forth from mission to community. It rests securely on the pivot of worship. If the pivot point is misplaced on something or someone else, mission and community fail miserably.

Church gatherings could start with a reminder of a believer's identity in Christ: fully forgiven, loved deeply, adopted without performance, and someone whom the Father is crazy about. With a reminder that our sin is laid upon Jesus (Isa. 53:6), we can establish equilibrium and fix our eyes on a God to be adored and magnified.

A problem arises when we call people to mission and community without establishing this gospel equilibrium first.

How will you coach a person to focus on gospel worship and identity?

4 PERFORMANCE-CENTERED LEADERSHIP

Leadership of yourself is even more challenging than leading others. But you cannot lead other's lives if you are not leading your life. Most people do not understand this concept. The next two chapters will focus on how we are prone to lead (through performance) and how we are designed to lead (through relationships).

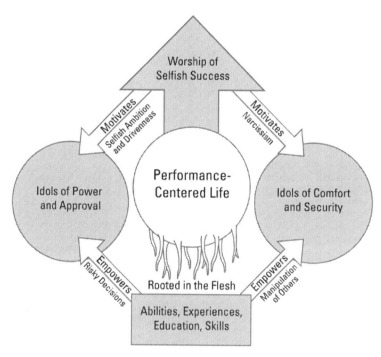

Performance-Centered Leaders Unhealthily Strive for Success through Driven Behaviors and Self-Absorption.

Christian leaders are known for their results—even among other believers. This is unfortunate because it is not how God accepts us. Tim Keller said it best:

> Do you realize that it is only in the gospel of Jesus Christ that you get the verdict before performance? The atheist and the Buddhist gets their verdict from performance. In Christianity, the verdict leads to performance...the moment we believe, God says, "This is my beloved son in whom I am well pleased."[18]

Christian leaders are getting their verdict from others through their performances, productivity, and "successes." Furthermore, leaders are finding their identity in *what they do*, rather than *who they are*. How many Christian leaders are sacrificing family, finances, physical and emotional health, and their souls to pursue success? I am afraid it is too common. LifeWay Research conducted a study of 1,000 protestant pastors in America that verified my hunch:

> A telephone survey of more than 1,000 senior pastors indicated a full 65 percent of them work 50 or more hours a week – with 8 percent saying they work 70 or more hours. Meetings and electronic correspondence consume large amounts of time for many ministers, while counseling, visitation, family time, prayer, and personal devotions suffer in too many cases.[19]

> ## I worked hard and long, not in rhythm to God's plan, but to be worthy of love.

I learned to work hard from both of my parents. God ordained mankind to work. It is God's plan, and it is good. But I worked hard to prove my worth. I do not remember ever receiving love from anyone that was devoid of my performance. So I worked hard and long, not in rhythm to God's plan, but to be worthy of love. As a result, I worked non-stop in ministry. As a youth pastor, I worked 70-75 hours a week. As a senior pastor (setting my own hours) I worked 80, and leading an International church planting network, I worked 84 hours, seven days a week, 364 days a year. I took Christmas Day off, at least most of it. The more I produced, the more I felt I was worthy of admiration and love.

We coach disciples with the understanding that some of them are motivated by their self-glorifying success. As the diagram above illustrates, it results in an inordinate ambition and drive, and it results in narcissism—a social epidemic of our day. Narcissism is considered a "mental disorder characterized by extreme self-absorption, an exaggerated sense of self-importance, and a need for attention and admiration from others."[20]

Narcissus, distinguished for his beauty, in Greek mythology, fell in love with his own reflection in the still waters of a spring and killed himself.[21]

Why do you believe Christian leaders struggle with a performance-centered approach?[22]

_____
_____
_____
_____
_____
_____

Prayer of Repentance

From this day forward, Jesus, I relinquish control. I will rest in You and Your will to build Your Kingdom. I will enjoy every aspect of the journey on which You are taking me. I will worship You and glorify You by taking a Sabbath (including not worrying if You need my help on my day off). I do not have to prove my worth to You, others or, the most annoying of all, myself. I am declared righteous by the unmerited gift of Jesus. You love me in spite of my ongoing sins. Rather than killing myself in Your name, lead me to turn and see God's glory in You—especially when the demands of ministry come as an avalanche toward me.

If this resembles your life in any way, don't just read the prayer above, stop, and pray it.

Rooted in Abilities

Performance-centered leadership is rooted in the fleshly attributes of education, abilities, experience, and skills. These are not bad things, unless a person depends upon them, rather than Spirit-empowerment. I served in an organization that never prayed together—ever. A lot of discussion took place around branding, marketing, strategy, vision, and funding, but only prayed to close a meeting. The results of dependence upon fleshly skills are two things (illustrated in the graphic at the beginning of this chapter):

1. **Risky decisions**. Jesus warned against making decisions based upon our own abilities: "For which of you, desiring to build a tower, does not first sit down and count the cost, whether he has enough to complete it?" (Luke 14:28). People who depend on their own abilities have most often succeeded and attempt to do things without carefully considering what the Spirit is leading them to do, because the ministry is not *functionally* dependent upon the Spirit's empowerment.

2. **Manipulation of others**. Christian leaders have a tendency to see people as a means to their work and not as the work. We don't use people to get ministry done; we use ministry to get people done.[23] Jesus told Peter to demonstrate his love for Jesus by feeding God's sheep and tending God's lambs. He didn't say, "If you love me, build an organization."

The Outcomes of Performance-Centered Leadership are Four Source Idols

Jesus was led of the Spirit into the wilderness *to be tempted* of the Devil (Matthew 4:1-11). The writer of Hebrews tells us that Jesus "who in every respect has been tempted as we are, yet without sin (Heb. 4:15). Jesus did not have to experience *every* nuance of sin man would encounter, but he had to be tempted and victoriously conquer the four source idols of all sin.[24]

Idol	Jesus' Temptations in Matthew 4:1-11
1. Approval	"If you are the son of God…"
2. Comfort	"Command these stones to be turned to bread."
3. Security	"Throw yourself down" and call the angels to rescue."
4. Power	"Fall down and worship me" and rule over kingdoms.

Jesus summarized the defeat of these tempting idols of our heart:
Be gone, Satan! For it is written, 'You shall worship the Lord your God and him only shall you serve' (Matt. 4:11).
In what way do you need to implement this prayer? _____

_____

_____

5 COACHING IN FIVE KEY RELATIONSHIPS

Performance-centered leadership is **my** sin. I never hit the wall or exploded in anger. Instead, my soul effused slowly over the course of 30+ years of ministry, and I found myself spiritually and emotionally tired of the stress of the performance cycle that I inflicted upon myself. After extended reflection, I identified five things that can make or break me or any Christian leader. I sought to improve on these areas in ways that I could apply in my life. They are the five relationships of church leaders that we pray coaches will proactively monitor as we pursue a gospel-centered style of leadership.
1. Relationship with God
2. Relationship with Self
3. Relationship with Friends
4. Relationship with Spouse and Family
5. Relationship with Ministry Leaders

1. Relationship with God

Paul David Tripp claims that the ministry war is "fought on the field of your heart."[25] Shepherding others is not just what you do, but who you are. Jesus said, "Out of the abundance of the heart the mouth speaks" (Luke 6:45). If we are not diligent and purposeful, we can find ourselves in a relationship with God as a pseudo business partner.

Meditating on Scripture is an important part of this relationship with God. Praying is another. God speaks to us, and we respond in prayer. Leaders cannot let their dependence on prayer slip in favor of business principles. The Apostle Paul encouraged the Church at Corinth, "So we do

26

not lose heart. Though our outer self is wasting away, our inner self is being renewed day by day" (2 Corinthians 4:16). Renewal comes through daily reading and heeding of God's word.

It is interesting the answers that I get when I ask Christian leaders about how they are repenting, what they are learning from God's word, and about their spiritual disciplines. They always engage energetically because it is something they value, but spiritual disciplines are often found shoved to the back of a person's full agenda.

The first area where attention is given, where coaching is offered, and where sustainable fruitful ministry takes place is the disciple's relationship with God. Paul urged servants of Jesus Christ to "train yourself for godliness" (1 Tim. 4:7). We all need people around us to help us to model this in a sustainable way.

How do you personally nurture your relationship with God (be specific)?

_____

_____

_____

_____

_____

2. Relationship with Self

Four key areas that are consistently indicated by church planters and those who work with them are the following: time management, finances, loneliness, and vague boundaries. [26] These are all the results of poor self management.

"Burnout is the final penalty for those who care too much as a part of their job," says Archibald Hart, professor of psychology, Fuller Theological Seminary. Hart went on to say:

> Burnout is a syndrome of emotional exhaustion, depersonalization, and reduced personal accomplishment that can occur among individuals who do people work of some kind. It is a response to the chronic, emotional strain of dealing extensively with people.[27]

In other words, Hart suggests that ministry can be harmful to your health. Developing a healthy relationship with self is an important part of shepherding the church of God.

Christians must personally take responsibility for their own selves (Acts 20:28). It is emotionally immature to assume the "church" or ministry organization is going to take care of the needs of the leader.

I am convinced that we need to be more aggressive about our needs and less dependent upon others to carry that burden for us. I am of the "ask, seek, knock" approach. I need to **ask** God in prayer to intervene and to sovereignly meet a need that I have. Then I began to **seek** solutions. I use my imagination and I try to be creative, thoughtful, strategic, and contemplative, all while emptying myself of my own will. Finally, I **knock** on the door of others and express the need in a straightforward manner. This takes the "passive" out of passive-aggressive. The leader is responsible for their needs, not their employing body or local church benevolence team.

The community can come alongside the leader and encourage and equip them, but that burden rests on the shoulders of the leader. The sooner our ministry leaders learn this, the healthier they will be. A right relationship with self demands that we develop self-care skills.

Self-care skills include a disciple's education, physical health, financial health, emotional health, schedule, and his relationships. I could talk about every one of these and I could give examples of how I failed at one point in all of these areas. One of the areas I see obliterated by Christian leaders, however, is the fourth commandment: remembering the Sabbath.

Why is the Sabbath forgotten so easily among church leaders?

_____

_____

_____

_____

_____

I read several books lately that flashed the yellow light of caution for ministers remembering the Sabbath. Leaders want to practice a consistent Sabbath, but think they are too essential to what God is going to accomplish in their local setting, said Paul Tripp, in his book _Dangerous Calling_. Tripp further said that this tendency leads to taking on more work than we are able to handle. Tripp said that he experienced this personally, "I begin to load the burden of the individual and collective growth of God's people onto my own shoulders."[28]

Whether we are doctors, lawyers, or [pastors], most of us today work too much, said Matthew Sleeth, a medical doctor who wrote _24/6: A Prescription for a Healthier, Happier Life_. He claimed that work is up 15 percent and leisure is down 30 percent and predicted that things will only get worse.[29] Hart added, "Pastors need to build recovery time into their life after every period of stress. Failure to do so means the body never catches up; it never heals itself and gets back to its original state. It is extremely important to respect the Sabbath."[30] An athlete must give their body time to heal itself after an intense workout. One workout resource explained how vital rest is to the body.

> It is rest that makes you stronger, because it is the rest that allows the muscles that you have broken down to heal and recover. It is the rest that allows you to recover so you can be strong, and thereby handle the increased weight, and increased number of sets and reps needed to gain further.[31]

In other words, unless we rest—particularly after a stressful event, we will eventually be weaker and less productive and less beneficial to the Kingdom.

I dishonored the Sabbath for years, heck, decades. "[A Sabbath] will happen only as a result of a conscious choice," said Sleeth[32] Peter Scazzero, in *Emotionally Health Church Planting* described a Sabbath as 52 God-given snow days. The key to a Sabbath is "to allow God to have the room, space, and quiet needed to make an impression on you" (Sleeth, 2012). The three R's of a Sabbath are rest, renewal, and reverence.

What would it look like if you and your family remembered the Sabbath consistently?[33]

_____

_____

_____

_____

_____

Self-management is the holistic care for your needs with a motivation to be healthy in every area of your life, and not just productive or approved. The first motivation brings glory to God; the latter may only bring glory to self.

3. Relationship with Friends

H.B. London, head of pastoral ministries for Focus on the Family disclosed that at least 70 percent of pastors in the United States claim they have no friends.[34] That is an alarming statistic. Some leading pastors advocate that a pastor should not pursue relationships with friends in their church. Pastors may be afraid to have friendships, especially if others have burned them in the past. This reticence for meaningful relationships leads to more loneliness and may lead to moral failure, burnout, or depression, according to Thom Ranier, President and CEO of LifeWay Christian

Resources.[35] C.S. Lewis wrote in *Four Loves* about the folly of protecting ourselves from broken hearts:

> To love at all is to be vulnerable. Love anything and your heart will be wrung and possibly broken. If you want to make sure of keeping it intact you must give it to no one, not even an animal. Wrap it carefully round with hobbies and little luxuries; avoid all entanglements. Lock it up safe in the casket or coffin of your selfishness. But in that casket, safe, dark, motionless, airless, it will change. It will not be broken; it will become unbreakable, impenetrable, irredeemable. To love is to be vulnerable.[36]

Three Types of Friendships

Ministry leaders seem to have three types of friendships: 1) Mentor friendships where we are investing time for the advancement of other people, 2) Mentee friendships where we are the recipients of others pouring into us, and 3) Mutual Friendships. I had more mentor friendships than anything else. It is not healthy for you to exclusively have mentor relationships. When you experience a need, the mentees will not feel compelled toward exercising a mutual friendship.

The three types of friendships:
1. **Mentor**
2. **Mentee**
3. **Mutual**

Both mentor and mentee relationships are draining on us. Mutual friendships benefit both parties. These are the kind of relationships we want to develop. In these relationships, we "exhort one another every day, as long as it is called 'today, that none of you may be hardened by the deceitfulness of sin" (Hebrews 3:13).

How will you pursue mutual relationships?

_____

_____

_____

_____

We need friends who love us sacrificially and unconditionally; friends we can trust and with whom we can just be ourselves. These are the kinds of relationships as C.S. Lewis describes where, "You have not chosen one another, but I have chosen you for one another."[37] These are relationships where we walk away filled, rather than emptied, or exhausted. Every ministry leader needs these mutual friendships in their life.

4. Relationship with Spouse and Family

The Christian leader's family is under attack. I am regularly counseling someone in a leader's family: husband, wife, kids, and even grown PK's. Recently, Jeannie and I spent about five hours talking with a husband and his wife convincing them that they should not quit ministry. At one point his voice, exhausted from the fight, dropped and said, "I might as well become a bartender, pausing, he added, "at a strip club." He then said, oddly, "where my wife could also work." I laughed along with him (hoping it was a joke); even though I could tell he was hurting so much that he could only envision the worst outcome for their lives. The following evening she wrote us an email thanking us for our investment in them and that the Spirit showed up in a huge way in their difficult situation.

Healthy ministries are led by those who have healthy marriages

The marriage and family relationship has huge ramifications for the mission of the church. The family dynamic is both the qualifying relationship for an elder and it is a pattern for church leadership. Paul said, "If someone does not know how to manage his own household, how will he care for God's church?" (1 Tim. 3:5).

> # We cannot expect the leader to be strong if the home is weak.

In coaching, the marriage and family is an issue that cannot be ignored, assumed, or glossed over. It affects every other area of a leader's life. We want to coach the planter as a spouse, a parent, and to understand and execute the biblical roles in the home. We want to support the pastor's spouse and provide couple coaching for leaders. We also want to support the pastor's kids (PK's). I engaged about 30 PK's this past summer. Some of them—many of them—are still reeling from the effects of their family serving the church. We need a new generation of PK's who love both Christ and His bride, the church.

Coaching can—and probably should—include financial coaching: how to develop a budget, how to get out of debt, and long-range planning. I see a huge need with Christian leader's families understanding how to serve Christ vocationally and to honor Christ in their families.

5. Relationship with Ministry Leaders

We relate to God, to self, to friends, to spouse and family, and we also need to develop a relationship with those we lead. This encompasses organizational leadership, team leadership, and pastoral leadership. Think about it. Many of us were told to lead with vision, with inspiration, with skill, with position, or even with force. But, we are rarely told to lead relationally. This is a mistake that many Christian leaders make. Jesus led through the relationships he had with the disciples. John often referred to himself as "the disciple whom Jesus loved." Barnabas led through relationships. Barnabas was a nickname given by the disciples that meant "son of encouragement." It was Barnabas that brought Saul to the Apostles. He had enough respect with the Apostles that they trusted him to bring this murder of Christians accomplice into their midst. The Apostle Paul led through relationships to Timothy and Titus.

Having a relationship means that we appropriately and biblically work through the variety of emotions that we inevitably experience with the people that we are called to lead and manage. Things rarely (never?) go the way we envision. Relationships will break down. Limited resources will be stressful. Leaders are misunderstood in multiple ways and multiple times. When leaders are perceived to have dropped the ball in any area, people treat them as if they should know better, so they often attack them behind their back instead of dealing with them biblically. The biblical response is to directly and privately ask what the leader meant or why a leader was motivated to act in a certain way. That could easily solve most conflicts. But most people choose "fight or flight." It's hard work to lead by relationship, but it is a biblical way.

It is vital for ministers to manage their ministry relationships. The spouse is equally affected by these *fight or flight* experiences. When our emotions experience nerve damage, we generally turn on each other as a married couple. It happens too easily and too often. When I see a pastor experiencing long-term stress, I focus on the marriage first and then the relationships with the leaders. My goal is to set up the police barriers first before dealing with the source of the stressors.

What kind of relationship issue with ministry leaders have you encountered in the last month?

_____

_____

_____

_____

How can the gospel address that relational issue?

_____

_____

_____

_____

_____

Relationships and the Gospel

God entered into a relationship with us through Christ. All of life will include some type of relationship. "God is relational," writes Vaughn Roberts. "He created us in his image as relational beings."[38] Healthy individuals are the result of healthy relationships. The opposite is also true. Where unhealthy relationships exist, an unhealthy person is always found— often either in the corner hiding or in the center fighting. The gospel restores our relationship with God and with others. Look at how the gospel is at the center of these relationships that leaders face.

1. Relationship with God

Because of the atoning death, burial, and resurrection of Christ, we have access to a relationship with God (Eph. 2:18). We are no longer illegitimate children; no longer enemies (John 8:41). We are sons of God and joint heirs with Jesus Christ John 1:12-13).

2. Relationship with Self

Our new identity is in Christ and therefore, we have peace with God and peace within ourselves. We no longer have to perform for our acceptance and there will no longer be any condemnation to those who are in Christ Jesus (Romans 8:1). This allows us to be people of rest, not those who are restless about approval from the Father.

3. Relationship with Friends

The resurrection of Jesus has broken down the middle wall of partition with God and with others (Eph. 2:13-22). Through Christ's incarnation, we are no longer called servants, but friends (John 15:15; Luke 12:4).

4. Relationship with Spouse and Family

The gospel of Jesus Christ is expressed profoundly through the church, the bride of Christ and the groom, Jesus Christ (Mark 2:19-20). This is a great mystery (Eph. 5:25-27). It was though the context of a family that all nations were blessed (Gen. 12:2-3; 18:18; 22:18). Through Christ we are members of the household of God (Eph. 2:19).

5. Relationship with Ministry Leaders

Jesus Christ was sent to seek and to save the lost (Luke 19:10). After His resurrection, he called the believers to go to all nations as his ambassadors (Matt. 28:16-20) and his ascension left the Holy Spirit to dwell with us and to empower us to be his witnesses—his proclaimers of the reality of his death and resurrection and his kingdom and sovereign rule—to the ends of the earth (Acts 1:8).

Reflect on one of the five relationships above. How can the gospel be applied immediately in your life?

_____

_____

_____

_____

_____

What would prevent you from applying the gospel to that relationship?

_____

_____

_____

_____

_____

6 COACHING LEADERS

We cannot coach everyone. We have to discern who God desires us to coach in this season of our ministry and life. Jesus chose Twelve to be His disciples (Mark 3:13-19; Luke 6:13-16). Barnabas traveled to Tarsus in search of Paul (Acts 11:19-26). Paul chose Timothy with recommendations from the Church at Lystra (Acts 16:1-3). We have to choose carefully those we will disciple.

The extent of coaching may be much larger than you imagined. The illustration below expresses the wide landscape of coaching possibilities.[39]

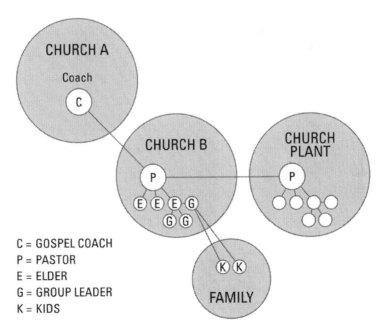

C = GOSPEL COACH
P = PASTOR
E = ELDER
G = GROUP LEADER
K = KIDS

When one of my sons was 20 years old, he came into our bedroom at 11:30 at night. He always knew he could talk to us at any time of the night. He plopped himself in the chair next to my side of the bed and said, "Coach me." In essence, he was saying that he didn't need quick answers or advice. He wanted to walk through the process of decision-making by my asking him insightful questions—well, as insightful as they can be at that time of night. These coaching principles can apply in multiple contexts.

> You then, my child, be strengthened by the grace that is in Christ Jesus, and what you have heard from me in the presence of many witnesses entrust to faithful men who will be able to teach others also. - 2 Timothy 2:2

How can 2 Timothy 2:2 help inform us *who* to coach?

_____

_____

_____

_____

Every person can coach 4 people:

- Week 1: Coach disciples 1 & 2
- Week 2: Coach disciples 3 & 4
- Week 3: Coach disciples 1 & 2
- Week 4: Coach disciples 3 & 4

Commitment: ~2 hours a Week
Investment: Four Transformed Lives

I believe every person can coach four people. Some will be able to do more. The time commitment is minimal if you follow the plan described in Gospel Coach. My current coaching load is 14 people. I allot 60 minutes for each coaching session for men and 90 minutes for women. Going longer can be counterproductive. I start on time and end on time. On occasion, a disciple will ask me permission to go longer. I have found that if the disciple's time is respected, they will reciprocate. I make every effort to be available to those I am coaching. At times, I have added a third or fourth session in the month to address an urgent or timely need they were facing.

The Coaching Session

- 15 minutes prior to the session, I review the answers submitted and pray for the upcoming session.

- **Connect** - Five minutes of the beginning of the call is connecting relationally. Women will need 15 minutes for this. I try to interact relationally at non-coaching times so that our coaching sessions do not feel rushed.

- **Review** - Five minutes reviewing prior session notes and follow up. This is important, although it might feel unproductive at first.

- **Objective** - Five minutes identifying the main objective for the coaching session at hand. The questions and answers exchanged between coach and disciple accelerates this. Sometimes I will identify the chief complaint and say, "It seems as though your main issue today is XYZ. Is that something you would like to discuss today?" Women may need ten minutes.

- **Strategy** - Thirty to thirty-five minutes is set aside to find appropriate strategies for their main objective. This is primarily where I ask questions. I take notes here so that they can talk freely and I can follow along by listening to the main ideas. Women can interact longer, but no longer than 40 minutes.

- Five minutes is reserved for recording points of accountability and action steps related to our coaching session.

- **Spirit & Supplication** - Five to seven minutes is given for prayer and asking the Spirit to empower the disciple to act on the coaching session. At times we will both pray. Often, this is where I pray for the disciple. I try to be specific about the coaching session issues.

- The final three to five minutes is making sure the next two coaching sessions are set. This is very important. It can be frustrating to try to coordinate calendars through email without an agreed upon time and place.

- After the session, I take five minutes to finish my notes on the session. I often add the new session to our shared Evernote Notebook. This is where I can add questions that we may not have addressed but can be discussed next time.

It is important to conduct a coaching session that is not robotic and stiff. The disciples should not even be aware of the shifts. It will be mechanical when you first start coaching, but will become dynamic, fluid, and Spirit-directed as you gain experience.

Never, Ever...

- Coach a person of the opposite gender unless it is a spouse or close relative.
- Expect that you cannot form an emotional and spiritual bond with a person you are shepherding.
- Spit in the wind
- Wear a sweater vest to preach.

I was asked about coaching a person with same sex attraction. I am not as inclined to say "Thou shalt not" here for three reasons. First, it is naïve to think that every person with same sex attraction is looking for a physical encounter or romantic relationship. Secondly, mutual attraction is not as applicable, in most cases, as it could be in a opposite gender coaching relationship. Finally, people with same sex attraction need good role models for what a healthy masculine or feminine relationship looks like.

Applications for Coaching:

- Coach Leaders
- Formal Discipleship
- Mentor in Specific Skills (church planting, groups, hospitality team, etc)
- Couples Coaching
- Leadership Development
- Supervisor
- Your context: _____

Coaching leaders is the obvious context for most coaching. You could use the context of coaching for formal discipleship. While most people agree that discipleship is not taking a person through a 8-week curriculum, you could use the principles of coaching to formalize a disciple-making relationship with someone. Coaching can be used to mentor another person in a skill. I used it to develop a small groups leader and I used it to train church planters. I also used it in a seminary cohort. Coaching can be used to shepherd a couple in ministry. In many contexts, the pastor is coached, but the spouse is left on their own. This application could help the couple in the myriad of coaching issues they face together as a couple and family while serving in ministry. This is especially true in church planting. You can decide what contexts you can utilize these newfound coaching skills.

Three Ways to Coach

1 = Individual

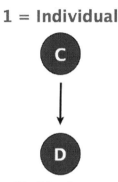

45-60 minutes

The first way to coach is **individual coaching**. This is going to be the majority of your coaching relationships. In the Gospel Coach model, you are going to be asking questions that require confidentiality in a private setting. You are inquiring of their personal lives and asking probing questions that may not be answered honestly in any other setting.

Another advantage with individual coaching is the exclusive and focused coaching that the disciple will receive. All of the 45 to 60 minutes is dedicated to helping them.

The second way to coach is in a **mentor coaching relationship**. In this relationship, the coach is typically a skilled, experienced, or educated leader who can mentor the disciples that are in a similar stage, affinity or ministry.

We did this in a pastor's training program where all of the disciples were at a similar stage of their church plant. The disciples gather in the same room and the coach spends 20 minutes coaching disciple #1 while the other two disciples listen

2 = Mentor

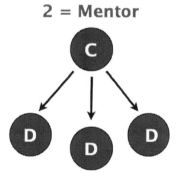

20 minutes each

intently and take notes. The other disciples do not interject thoughts unless asked. After 20 minutes, the second disciple is coached while the other two listen in. This can work with three church planters, elders in training, small group leaders, missionaries, project team members, seminary students, or women's ministry leaders. It does not work well if one is a church planter, another a women's ministry leader, and the last one the financial manager. They have to have some similar level of interest or involvement.

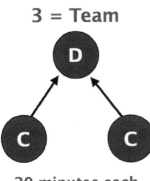

3 = Team

20 minutes each

The third way to coach is **Team Coaching**. This is a fun way to coach one another. In this format, two people are coaching one disciple. They both ask questions and walk through whatever need the disciple is facing. After twenty minutes, the table is turned and a different person is coached by the other two coaches. This style is a great way to learn how to coach.

This works best if all three of the participants are at a similar level of development. If one of them is advanced in experience, education, or skill, the group will revert to a mentor coaching style deferring to the senior leader in the group.

The participants in this style can enter into a covenant together and thus engage in issues that are typically the topics handled at the individual coaching level. This is a great way to build a team with mutual vulnerability, unity, critical thinking, and faith-filled actions.

Practice Team Coaching:

Choose two other people and practice this style of coaching. Use the question (or variation), "What is the biggest challenge you are facing in your job?"

Think of four to six people who you could coach. Pray and discern who you will coach.

1. _____
2. _____
3. _____
4. _____
5. _____
6. _____

The easiest way to approach someone is to ask them to help you in learning how to coach: "Will you help me to complete a coach training certification and to learn how to coach?" They won't expect too much from you!

You can also look for those people in your sphere of oversight. For example, if you are leading a group, choose one or two from the group that you can disciple. If you are a pastor, select a staff person or a prominent leader or elder.

Why does every church leader need a coach?[40]

_____

_____

_____

_____

_____

_____

_____

_____

7 COACHING CONVERSATION

Coaching is an intentional gospel conversation with focused discussions about a disciple's personal, spiritual, and missional life. This is the key statement about Gospel Coach. The book is really an attempt to lay the foundation for this statement and then explain how it is practiced. If you understand this statement, you understand Gospel Coach.

The conversation is the basis for the coaching relationship. It has all of the elements of a normal conversation with a few nuances and emphases.

Intentional Conversation

First, coaching is an intentional interaction with defined roles between two or more people: coach and disciple. It is fine to have coffee with friends, but coaching is much more than just meeting together for a set time frame. Coaching is meeting with an agreed upon agenda resulting in action items and life transformation.

Gospel Conversation

Secondly, it is a gospel conversation. This does not mean that we only talk about the gospel. It means that we have a conversation about the disciple's life and we apply the gospel to areas where they are "not acting in line with the truth of the gospel" (Gal. 2:14, NIV). We are not the sin police as coaches, we are looking for grace in their life. However, idols of power, approval, comfort, or security may be exposed in normal conversation. For example, my friend struggled with a security idol his whole life. He talked with me about how his life would be wasted if he lost the grip on his failing marriage. Our conversation about everyday life led us to the gospel. I tried to coach him through the truth of the sovereignty of God who was the only one with full control.

Focused Discussions

Thirdly, it is a discussion focused on the disciple. Conversations are often reciprocal where one shares while the other listens and then the roles change. In coaching, the focus is on the disciple. It does not mean that the coach cannot share, but rather that the coach only shares what is necessary to connect relationally. When I talk to a leader that mentions their child, I might mention that I have two sons, but I don't bust out the pictures and the stories—even if I want to share. My wife coached a woman who was complaining about not keeping up with the home responsibilities with four rambunctious kids. She said, "One day they won't be there to make messes and you will wish their toys were strewn all over the floor. Now, let's talk about how you can enjoy these years without complete frustration."

Personal, Spiritual, and Missional Life[41]

Chapter five of *Gospel Coach* explains this in detail. This is a matrix for getting from casual conversations to gospel conversations. Essentially I wanted to go from only talking about a golf trip to Scotland with Pastor Ty toward a gospel application in his troubled marriage. I imagined how conversations over coffee could naturally be led through this matrix.

I always start with the personal dimension in coaching. I then ask questions about their spiritual journey. We all have one, even if we do not have a relationship with God through Jesus. Finally, I ask questions about their vocational and/or missional life.

I aim for 50% of the conversation dealing with the missional or vocational life of a person. At times, another dimension, spiritual or personal, is more demanding and should consume a greater portion. The percentage is merely a guide. Acts 20:28 instructs to pay careful attention to yourself and pay careful attention to the flock. This is how I view it:

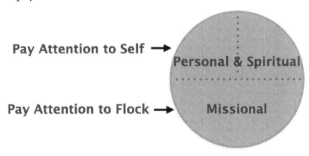

43

That's a Great Question!

Coaching is asking great questions. You will know it when they respond, "That's a great question." Appendix 2 and 4 of *Gospel Coach* are lists of coaching questions to get you started. If you have access to the book, look them over and answer the following question. If not, come up with your own questions.

What are some good coaching questions?[42]

_____

_____

_____

_____

_____

What makes a good coaching question?

_____

_____

_____

_____

_____

Tips for Asking Good Questions:

- As they discuss their challenge, assume the point of view of those they are interacting and ask the questions that naturally come to mind.
- Use the comments, "tell me more" and "What else?" to encourage them to explore their options and their hidden motives.
- Listen longer than you think is necessary. Listen until you are moved.

Listening is a diminishing skill. The greatest benefit Carl Rogers provided therapy (and by extension, coaching) is what he and Richard Farson called *active listening*. They claimed that sensitively listening with an interest in the speaker, rephrasing points of thought, and responding to feelings "brings about changes in people's attitudes toward people and themselves."[43]

Coaches have to learn to listen effectively to create learning environments that then facilitate the implementation of the strategies the disciples face. This empowers the disciple to make changes.[44]

Judi Brownell developed the HURIER model of listening as a theoretical base for developing listening skills. This model includes six components of listening (hearing, understanding, interpreting, remembering, evaluating, and responding):[45]

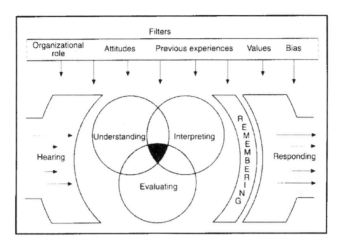

Hearing is the process of putting ourselves in an attitude to hear what the other person says. Providing questions to the disciple prior to the coaching session is a step in that direction. Sitting (in person, on screen, or on the phone) with the sole purpose of hearing what another person has to say can be transformative for both parties.

Understanding includes perceiving exactly what they are saying. Re-phrasing in your own words is a useful tool to make certain you are understanding what they are saying. Understanding may require researching and learning about what they are experiencing. For example, I coached a pastor who had two children who were born with spina bifida. I researched it after the first session so that I could somewhat mentally understand what he and his wife were experiencing.

Remembering is important so that the coach can recall past conversations and can help the disciple to make appropriate decisions. I find that taking notes in Evernote while I am coaching is very valuable. I create a shared Notebook for every disciple. I can make a new Note for every coaching session. I do not rely on my memory, especially if my coaching load is heavy.

Interpreting the verbal and nonverbal content in its context allows the coach to give feedback to the disciple. We have to interpret *what* is being said, as well as *how* it is being said. We also have to interpret the context and how changing dynamics alters the disciple's actions.

Evaluating is the process of verifying whether the disciple is expressing an accurate perception of their stated position. This takes time as the coach gets to know the disciple in a more holistic way. In a coaching session, a man offered a generous gift to another person. I told my wife about it (without sharing names) and she asked if he was just joking. To which I stated, "I am sure it was sincere because he doesn't ever joke about anything." My knowledge of him allowed me to evaluate quickly.

Responding is demonstrating to the disciple that the coach is energetically listening to them. Responses include nonverbal nods and verbal reactions: back-channeling (uh-huh, okay, etc.), paraphrasing, empathizing, supporting, analyzing, and advising.[46]

We can draw from Carl Rogers and Judi Brownell to come up with eight basic listening skills:

Listening 101

1. Maintain a posture of hearing and remove all distractions.
2. Listen longer than you think is necessary.
3. Show respect for them as you are listening carefully without pseudo listening.
4. Re-phrase their thoughts
5. Watch for non-verbal cues
6. Provide feedback on their feelings without interrupting. "It sounds like you are…"
7. Defer judgment.
8. Ask open-ended, probing questions.

I appreciate learning listening skills, but I am motivated in a profound way by understanding that my listening to others can display the Good News of Jesus Christ:

Listening is the Gospel on Display

- An act of grace extended to another
- An act of love to care for another
- An act of compassion
- An act of Holy Spirit partnership

When we listen to another person, we extend grace to them, although we do not have to listen. God does not have to extend His favor on us, yet, because of grace, He initiates favor toward us.

As we listen, we are making ourselves available for caring for the disciple. During that session, the things that matter to them are of utmost importance to us and we are investing our time and energy for their good.

Jesus saw the crowd of people and was moved with compassion because they were like sheep without a shepherd (Matt. 9). Listening puts us into a shepherding posture to compassionately serve another person.

The Spirit led Jesus throughout His ministry (Luke 4:1, 14, 18). As we listen to the disciple, we are to simultaneously listen to the Spirit. At times, we will not know how to respond to those we are coaching. When we allow ourselves to be Spirit-led in our coaching, we will give a response, feedback, or insight that brings gospel transformation to the disciple.

PRACTICE LISTENING. Ask someone to explain their top two challenges they are facing in their life. Implement the eight listening skills above. What did you learn from this listening exercise?

_____
_____
_____
_____
_____
_____

8 COACHING LIKE A SHEPHERD

Christian leadership is shepherding. A trend exists among large churches to excuse this language. One very prominent pastor was asked in an interview with Leadership Journal if we should stop comparing pastors to shepherds. He said, "Absolutely. That word needs to go away...It was culturally relevant in the time of Jesus, but it's not culturally relevant any more. This pastor believes that the "pastor as CEO" is a better model.[47]

I relate more closely to a CEO than a shepherd, but Christian leaders cannot choose which model best fits. We choose the one that Scripture chose. The Greek verb for shepherd, care, rule, or tend is poimainon. It is used in Acts 20:28, "*Care* for the church of God." The Greek noun for shepherd is poimen. Peter exhorts, "For you were straying like sheep, but have now returned to the Shepherd [poimen] and Overseer of your souls." - 1 Peter 2:25 (c.f. Matt. 26:31; John 10:11, 14, 16; Heb. 13:20).

Jesus said, "I am the good Shepherd [poimen]" (John 10:11, 14). Leaders in the church are the undershepherds and are told to "shepherd the flock of God that is among you" (1 Peter 5:2). John MacArthur explained:

> Church leaders are undershepherds who guard the flock under the Chief Shepherd's watchful eye (Acts 20:28). Theirs is a full-time responsibility because they minister to people who, like sheep, often are vulnerable, defenseless, undiscerning, and prone to stray.[48]

Coaching with a Shepherd's Posture

My relatives are real cowboys—not like the cowboys in Nashville, and certainly not like the naked cowboy in Manhattan!. My cousins raise cattle for a living. We spent a lot of time on their cattle ranch as kids. We watched our Uncles run their cows down a chute and into a truck to go to market. If one of the cows hesitated, she held up the whole herd and was encouraged to move along with the help of a cattle prod. Unfortunately, I chose this model of leading with an electrical shock to "encourage" church boards instead of applying shepherding principles. We got a lot of ministry done, but it was not consistent with biblical leadership.

Biblical Leadership:

- Know the Sheep
- Feed the Sheep
- Lead the Sheep
- Protect the Sheep

Tim Witmer (*The Shepherd Leader*, *The Shepherd Leader at Home*)

Coaching with a shepherd's posture starts with **knowing** and loving the sheep intimately. You cannot lead those you do not love. The majority of shepherding is spent feeding and leading. We **feed** and equip the disciple with God's word and with a focus on the gospel of Jesus Christ. We **lead** sacrificially as we oversee every area of a disciple's life with Spirit-empowered discernment. A shepherd takes the posture of "we" and walks alongside as a friend. The shepherd **protects** the disciple with Christ-like compassion, comfort, and fighting and defending against those things that attack the disciple.

Ten Qualities of a Gospel Coach

Shepherding Roles	Qualities of a Gospel Coach
Know the sheep	1. Relating personally
Feed the sheep	2. Nourishing with truth
	3. Inspiring toward Jesus
	4. Equipping in needs
Lead the sheep	5. Investing sacrificially
	6. Overseeing every aspect of a person's life
	7. Guiding with Spirit-empowered discernment
Protect the sheep	8. Displaying compassion
	9. Comforting with hope in the gospel
	10. Fighting for their good

EXERCISE:

Chapters 6 through 10 of *Gospel Coach* describe the ten qualities of coaching with the ancient posture of shepherding. Write out a one sentence explanation for each quality below:

Knowing

1. Relating Personally - _____
   _____

Feeding

2. Nourishing with Truth - _____
   _____

3. Inspiring toward Jesus - _____
   _____

4. Equipping in Needs - _____
   _____

Leading

5. Investing Sacrificially - _____
   _____

6. Overseeing every Aspect of a Person's Life - _____
   _____

7. Guiding with Spirit-Empowered Discernment - _____
   _____

Protecting

8. Displaying Compassion - _____
   _____

9. Comforting with Hope in the Gospel - _____
   _____

10. Fighting for their Good - _____
    _____

Describe an effective coach in any arena of life (sports, vocal, tutor, life, etc.):

_____
_____
_____
_____
_____

How do these characteristics compare with the ten Gospel Coach Qualities?

_____
_____
_____
_____
_____

Help the Disciple to Recognize the Sin beneath the Sin

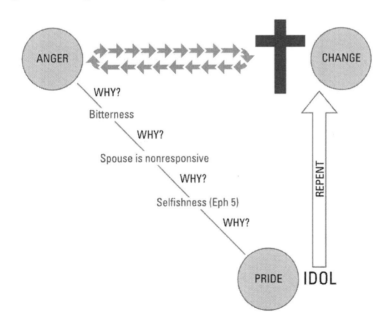

As the disciple confesses a sin, be patient and explore the *why* beneath the *what*. Continue digging as long as they are able. Together, find the root sin that is giving birth to surface sins. Jesus said, "But what comes out of the mouth proceeds from the heart, and this defiles a person" (Matt. 15:18).

Coaching as an Advisor or a Shepherd?

Advisor	Shepherd
1. I/You	1. We
2. Content-Based	2. Process-Based
3. Free-flow of Words	3. Filter (edit!)
4. Solution-Driven	4. Transformation-Driven
5. Speed Counseling	5. Hiking with a Friend
6. Helpful	6. Compassionate
7. Efficient	7. Thorough
8. Personal Experiences	8. Empathy
9. Hierarchical Roles	9. Friendship
10. Information/Speak	10. Inquiry/Listen
11. Convicting Tone	11. Encouraging Tone
12. Reform the Beliefs	12. Retell their Story
13. Direct Confrontation	13. Indirect Confrontation[49]
14. Narrow Applications	14. Deep Exploration
15. Self-assured	15. Humility

Look over the list above comparing an advisor role to a shepherd role.

- In what ways do you need to make adjustments in your approach to coaching?

- Which skill or practice above do you need to gain a better understanding?

- When are you most prone to lean toward advisor mode?

Accountability and Coaching

The purpose of a bridge is to get across a body of water; to get from point A to point B. That is the only purpose. The bridge has *accountability* based on the pillars. The pillars are not the purpose. The pillars provide integrity to the bridge for the purpose of getting to the other side. It is important to remember that accountability is not the purpose, but adds integrity as the disciple takes the small steps toward gospel transformation.

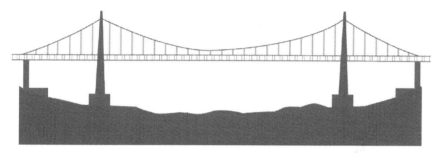

Accountability in coaching is a way to assist the disciple, not to attack them. The coach can make a file for coaching accountability. These are items that the disciple asks the coach to help them achieve. These can be goals or projects. They can be relational, moral, or behavioral. Every significant action that the disciple decides to accomplish could benefit from an accountability item. Accountability is controlled by disciple and monitored by the coach.

Accountability

1. Is not Defensive
2. Is not Deflecting
3. Is not Dishonest
4. Is not Distant
5. Is not Demeaning
6. Is not Demanding
7. Is not Deceiving

Five Basics for Accountability

1. Focus on your need for the gospel and your response to the grace of God.

2. Find people who have regular contact with you and can observe your life closely.

3. Find people who are not employed by you or under your direct authority. Sometimes silence on their part concerning your questionable behavior means not getting fired. It is okay to supplement your accountability with people under your supervision, but they cannot be the only ones who are holding you accountable.

4. Train your accountability team to ask hard questions and to be relentless about their receiving an accurate answer, even if it feels as thought they question your honesty. If you can lie to your accountability team, it is of no value or protection to you.

5. Utilize questions that are not the same every week and find questions that examine sins in your head and your heart and not just in your hands. I believe sin starts in our head where we entertain ungodly thoughts. If we do not take every thought captive, sin moves into our heart where we long to fulfill that lustful thought. Jesus spoke about this as he condemned, not only the act of adultery, but the heart's desire for adultery (Matt. 5:28). James said, "But each person is tempted when he is lured and enticed by his own desire. Then desire when it has conceived gives birth to sin, and sin when it is fully grown brings forth death" (James 1:15-16).

Read Acts 20:28-30 Carefully

"So guard yourselves and God's people. Feed and shepherd God's flock—his church, purchased with his own blood—over which the Holy Spirit has appointed you as elders. I know that false teachers, like vicious wolves, will come in among you after I leave, not sparing the flock. Even some men from your own group will rise up and distort the truth in order to draw a following" (Acts 20:28-30, NLT).

In what ways could your coaching be similar to shepherding others (Acts 20:28-30)?

_____

_____

_____

_____

_____

9 GOSPEL LIFE PLAN

I meet very few Christian leaders who have a plan for their life. Those who do have not engaged another person in the process so it often lacks the grounding it needs to become a useful tool. I believe three reasons exist why it is vital to have a coach walk through a Gospel Life Plan with a disciple. First, those self-generated life plans are often too vague. The Gospel Life Plan needs to be aspiring toward something we can actually visualize unfolding over time. Secondly, life plans are too short-sighted. It needs to guide us toward the end of our life, not just this month. Thirdly, it is not holistic. A life plan needs to address every area of our life: God, self (mental, physical, emotional, and relational), spouse, children, friends, vocation, finances, ministry.

Many business leaders urge people to establish goals. This is similar, but fundamentally different. The difference is where it starts. The Gospel Life Plan starts with God's calling on an individual, rather than on personal aspirations. This is an important key distinction.

The goal of this chapter is to help the coach to develop their Gospel Life Plan and secondly to be able to help a disciple to develop theirs. It would be absurd to expect a disciple to work on theirs if the coach has no interest. The only effective plan is one that is written down, monitored, revised when needed, and followed. The last one is the key followed.

The Gospel Life Plan (GLP) serves in a similar manner as a GPS device. Most people use their smart phone to navigate to an unknown location. It tells us where we are and how to get

there. It will also make adjustments if we get off-track. The GLP will guide your coaching sessions. With it in hand, you can ask if the disciple wants to get off course for a time period or if they want to follow the plan they have set for their life. It is a powerful tool, but should not be used manipulatively by the coach. It is to serve the disciple to help them achieve their calling.

Five Reason for Written Goals:

1. Clarifies your calling
2. Prioritizes your life
3. Motivates you toward action
4. Defense against quitting
5. Forces regular evaluation of desired outcomes

Living life without goals,
is like playing hockey with no puck.

Four Quadrants of a Gospel Life Plan[50]

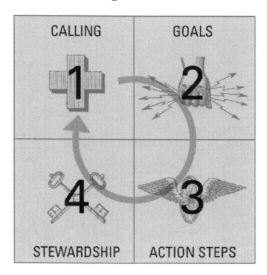

The *Gospel Life Plan* guides a disciple in all three dimensions in the coaching journey: personal, spiritual, and missional.

1. **Calling** (your mission, the ultimate *who*).

    The disciple-leader discerns their calling from God, the purpose or mission that defines their service to God. This can be a specific calling, like a calling to lead a small group, or a calling to start a church. It can also be a general calling as a Christian to live in community with others, to make disciples, to practice spiritual disciplines, and to exhibit fruits of the Spirit. This is as much *who* you are, than *what* you do.

Tim Keller describes a calling as the intersection of three elements. Keller believes all three must be in place to discern a calling. Answer these three questions:

- Passion – what is the specific passion God has placed on your heart?

- People – what credible people are affirming this calling?

- Place – what opportunities do you have to exercise this passion?

2. **Goals** (your vision, the exciting *what next*).

These are the high level, big picture goal(s) that a disciple-leader identifies that will enable them to accomplish that call. I call them the big bucket goals because if we try to carry too many buckets, we will spill it all.

We are told to find balance in life. But balance in life is never achievable and it is unnatural. Life has seasons and rhythms (Eccl. 3:1-8). We are not to be born and die, plant and uproot, weep and laugh at once; but at different seasons. For instance, we plow, then plant, then fertilize, then weed, then harvest, then eat, and then rest.

It is unreasonable to seek to be balanced with marriage, family, work, health, church, and community. You will drive yourself crazy with guilt, stress, and busyness if you try to do all at once in some kind of balance. Ask yourself, "What season is it?"

Use the table on the next page to begin listing some big goals in the three dimensions in this season of your life.

Personal Goals	Spiritual	Missional

3. **Action Steps** (your strategy, the simple *how*).

These are specific steps that a disciple-leader carries out, leading to the advancement of the goals. "Vision without execution is a daydream. Execution without vision is a nightmare."

Action steps begin with the end goal in mind. For instance, if the end goal is to raise $50,000 for a church plant, it starts with references, then casting vision, then establishing a bank and online website for online giving, then meeting 25 churches, then meeting 25 individuals. Unless you have specific and orderly action plans, you will never reach your goals.

References	Vision	Bank/Web	25 churches	25 Individuals	$50K

Use the chart below to think through the action steps for your goal. Start with the end in mind, the 6th slot.

1	2	3	4	5	6

4. **Stewardship** (your values, the compelling *why*).

    To avoid imbalance and unhealthy patterns, the advancement of the goals through specific steps of action is governed by whole–life stewardship of time, resources, abilities, relationships, experiences, and knowledge. You cannot do everything. To truly pursue your calling, you will have to place limitations on almost *every* area of your life.

Review Your Calling Regularly

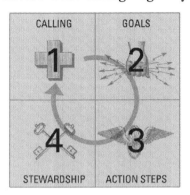

Notice that the arrow starts with calling and returns to that quadrant. It is important to regularly review your calling and thus amend your goals. I think it is important to review your calling every year. Your goals should be reviewed every quarter and your action steps at least every month to monitor progress. I keep my GLP on Evernote and I have access to it on my computer, my iPad and my iPhone. When I have to wait for an appointment, I will review my GLP on my phone.

Develop and Monitor Your Gospel Life Plan

Recently, Jeannie and I became empty nesters. Both of our sons moved out within three months of each other. One got married—and these newlyweds insisted on getting their own apartment, even though we had a perfectly good bedroom in our house for them to use! The other son moved back to Seattle to work and to go to school. Our life stage changed dramatically. I reviewed my GLP in light of this new stage of life and I made adjustments accordingly.

If you don't make adjustments as the landscape of your life changes, you will end up in a mess. On an episode of The Office, Dwight Schrute and Michael Scott religiously followed their GPS that was not updated and drove straight into a lake.

Dwight:	"This is the Lake!"
Michael:	"The Machine knows."
Dwight:	"This is the lake! This is the lake! There's no road here!"
Michael:	"Stop yelling at me! Stop yelling at me!" [Drives into lake]
Dwight:	"Remain calm. I have trained for this. Okay, exit the window! Here we go."
GPS:	[Garbled] "Make a U-Turn if possible."

It's Your Turn

On the next page, begin to complete your Gospel Life Plan. Use this to get started. Make bullet points of your big ideas. It may not be enough space to complete it, but it can get you started.

Plan a GLP Day. Go to a place where you can pray, read Scripture, think, and enjoy silence and solitude. Block out four hours for this. Some of you may want to spend more time. Meet a trusted friend for lunch, and share your insights with them. Let them evaluate it. In the afternoon, meet with two or three colleagues who can provide response. Finally, share it with your spouse and let them give feedback. After the evening meal, make the final draft in whatever format best suits you. Consider the words of Dorothy Canfield Fisher (1879-1958). Dorothy was named by Eleanor Roosevelt as one of the ten most influential women in the United States: [51]

> *You can't hit a target you can't see. If we would only give the same amount of reflection to what we want out of life that we give to the question of what to do with two week's vacation, we would be startled at our false standards and the aimless processions of our busy days.*
>
> *- Dorothy Canfield Fisher*

	Personal	Spiritual	Missional
Calling			
Goals			
Action Steps			
Stewardship			

10 COACHING WITH THE C.R.O.S.S.

It all comes together here. All of the previous chapters will come alive in the following pages. The goal here is to explain how the coaching session actually takes place. With a grasp of the gospel, a posture as a shepherd, and some tools in hand, you are ready to start coaching.

Tom Wood developed a useful tool for the process of coaching that he calls C.R.O.S.S. Many people tell me that this has been very helpful to have some structure to their coaching.[52]

C.R.O.S.S. Coaching

C – Connect
R – Review
O – Objective
S – Strategies
S – Supplication and Spirit

The structure needs to exist without being seen. It is like a skeleton that is necessary for the human body, but nobody want to see one. I am going to chronologically walk through the coaching session in a very practical manner.

C – Connect

The first letter in C.R.O.S.S. is *"Connect."* We want to connect to the disciple, to the gospel, and to the Spirit of God who will guide us and teach us in all truth. Connect is where we exercise the shepherding skill of *knowing*. We will look at connecting by establishing a coaching relationship and then explore how we connect at each subsequent session.

Establishing a Coach-Disciple Relationship

Once you have prayed about who you believe God is leading you to coach, approach them with the idea. Here is where most relationships break down. I see adults who shy away from these disciple-making relationships like a junior high kid. Check the box if you like me. Scripture commands us to make disciples and it also implores us to teach one another (Titus 2). We have younger people waiting for older people to approach them and we have older people waiting to be asked. Again, it's like a junior high dance and everyone is drinking the punch instead of dancing. Older man or woman, go ask that young person that the Spirit has placed on your heart. Younger man or woman, go ask that person if they will coach you.

Share the coaching covenant. This is found in Appendix 1 in *Gospel Coach*. Essentially, it outlines the time frame, agenda, and expectations. Set up your first two appointment dates.

The coach can then send the Intake Form questions. This is found in Appendix 2 of *Gospel Coach* where I wrote 130 questions that you can choose from that work best for your situation. I personally do not ask more than 20 questions in my Intake Form. I don't want it to feel like an application to law school.

I ask the people I am coaching to do an abbreviated (and free) DISC test that is found online.[53] I include it with the Intake Questions. It gives me some understanding of their personality profile and informs me how to best communicate to them. PeopleKeys states, "A DISC Profile utilizes a method for understanding behavior, temperament, and personality. It provides a comprehensive overview of the way that people think, act, and interact. It is the most widely used profiling tool of its kind, and is supported by decades of validation and reliability studies."[54]

At the first coaching session, my goal is to get to know them better, identify some issues, and to develop trust. I always express total confidentiality in our coaching sessions. I want the disciple to feel free to share anything with me that will help them. If I feel they need to confess something to a spouse or to an employer, it is not my responsibility to expose their behavior unless they threaten to physically hurt themselves or another person. I shepherd the disciple through what is best to do in those situations. I have not had anyone refuse to confess what we determined would be the Biblical course of action. My role as coach in these instances becomes biblical peacemaker. The first question a disciple asks is, "Can I trust you?" One indicator of the established trust is when they say, "I cannot believe I am telling you this."

Establishing a relationship with a disciple looks like the following:

CONNECT

- Identify and invite the disciple.
- Share Coaching Covenant
- Set up the initial two appointments
- Send approximately 20 Intake Questions by email
- Pre-read their answers
- Pray for the disciple
- First Session

First Session

The first session will feel differently than the other sessions. Getting to know them is the goal. If you think that you already know them, you will be surprised the things that you learn in this more formalized relationship. You will know them at a greater level whereby you can help them better as you embark in this journey together.

The questions you send can be done in one of several ways. You can send the questions through email at least a week prior to your meeting. You could use Google Drive and share a Word document. We are building a website to serve as a place to coach. Until it is built, I am using Evernote. I have a premium account so that I can share a Notebook with the disciple and they can answer them. We can both see the Notebook at any time. I like that I can operate it on my computer, my iPad, or my iPhone. I make a separate Notebook for every coaching relationship and share it with them:

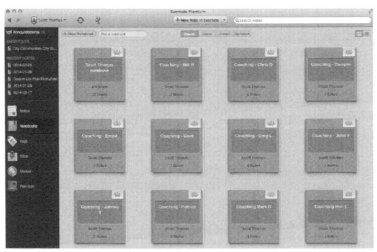

I write questions in the shared Notebook and the disciple gets a notice on their computer that the Notebook has been updated. I place a bullet point under each question where they can easily answer. They answer the questions at their leisure and I get them on my devices.

The benefit of having this in your smart phone device is that you can pray for them and think about how to best serve them at all times. I have added questions or comments to their Notes while waiting for a traffic light. The guy behind me let me know when it turned green!

During the actual coaching session, the coach can capture the notes. One quirk of Evernote is that only one person at a time can make additions to the Note. However, once you have both sync'd the app, either can take notes. I prefer to take notes because it helps me to listen more carefully so that I can capture the most salient points. The disciple is then unencumbered to interact.

Connect in Subsequent Sessions

You will want to approach every coaching relationship as a journey of two friends with a mission in mind—brothers on mission together. The mission of personal, spiritual, and missional health drives the agenda and should dominate the percentage of your time spent together. But you will want to connect relationally every time you meet. For some coaches, this is easier than others and you will need to discipline yourself so that it is not just two friends having coffee together. The coach carries this responsibility to get to the agenda in appropriate time, without feeling rushed to "check off" the connect part of coaching.

I usually will not spend more than the first five minutes connecting. Normally, I will have connected with them in between sessions and therefore, I do not have to start over each time. I have one pastor that I coach that cherishes this connecting time and I simply build in extra time to the session. He would feel short-changed if we didn't connect in a significant manner.

This connect phase includes connecting to the Spirit and to the gospel. You can do this naturally by saying something like, "We have some heavy issues to discuss today. Let's pray and ask the Spirit of Truth to give us insight for these issues today." You don't have to say some special words or raise your hands (unless you want). You simply invite the Spirit to guide, teach, comfort, convict, reveal, and empower your session.

Be careful not allowing the coaching sessions to turn into friends having coffee. The disciple/pastor/pastor's spouse/leader has ample opportunity for friendships. But coaching sessions are rare. Protect them for the advancement of the Kingdom.

Shepherding Roles	Personally	Spiritually	Missionally
Know the sheep	How did you become a Christian?	What is God doing in your heart right now?	What opportunities have you had for sharing your faith?
Feed the sheep	What is God teaching you about your role as a husband and father/wife and mother/single person?	What information or resources would be helpful for your spiritual growth?	What resources do you need to accomplish your ministry goals?
Lead the sheep	How are you personally leading others in your family?	How is the Lord leading you to respond to him?	What is the mission of your ministry?
Protect the sheep	What temptations occur in your personal life?	What priority do you give to Bible reading and prayer in your life?	Where are you prone to waste time in ministry?

Choose one of the CONNECT questions above and ask another person.

R – Review

The second letter in C.R.O.S.S. is *"Review."* This will take no more than five minutes normally. The questions sent ahead of time facilitate the quick review. On your first session, you will look over the answers as your review. Subsequent sessions will also have some follow-up items for your review. It would be helpful to look at past sessions and review any items that were noted as actionable or serious. For instance, "Last time, you mentioned that your daughter was going in for an exam. What were the results?" You might also ask this in your pre-questions.

When I ask questions, I focus on the five relationships explained in a previous chapter of this workbook. Below are some sample questions.

REVIEW Questions

- How is your relationship with God?
- How did you Sabbath this past week?
- In what ways have you pursued mutual friendships?
- Describe your relationship with your spouse (if applicable) or parents. What challenges are you facing with your children (if applicable)?
- How are your relationships at work/school?

Choose one of the REVIEW questions above and ask another person. What did you experience?

_____
_____
_____
_____
_____

The other thing that you will want to review is their accountability items. These are things that they have asked you to help them to achieve. The coach does not assign accountability items. If you don't bring them up, they may not offer that information and it will be of no use to them. I make a separate Notes file in the shared coaching Notebook that is entitled "accountability." This is where I can record any actionable items. I can capture them right at the moment and the disciple can see them in their Notebook. Once they are completed, I can delete it or move it to a file called "Completed Accountability." This provides a record of wins.

I always try to include evidences of God's grace as a review inquiry. By asking them how God is working in their life, it forces them to remember and praise Him for His provision. If we are not careful, we can spend all of our coaching time examining what is broken. This provides a much-needed grace perspective.

The pinnacle of the review time is the identification of the objective for the coaching session. This is the mutual identification of one or two major issues to focus for this meeting.

REVIEW Summary

- Send questions prior to the session.
- Prayerfully review the answers.
- Were there any issues from last session?
- Review the Accountability Items
- Inquire of God's active working in their life.
- Identify one or two items to discuss.

O – Objective

The third letter in C.R.O.S.S. is "*Objective*." This is the most important aspect of the coaching session, but should take no more than five minutes normally. This is identification of what physicians refer to as the "chief complaint." The objective is the primary concern for that coaching session. This is not the objective for life, but rather, for that coaching session.

The coach will undoubtedly have to help the disciple to identify this session objective. An objective a clearly defined objective and should be tied to the disciple's Gospel Life Plan. An example of a good objective would be the following:

- Starting five new missional communities inside the city limits by the end of the year to disciple 50 people.
- Training 30 women in Gospel Coach by the end of August.

SMART Objectives:

- Is it **SPECIFIC**?
- Is it **MEASURABLE**?
- Is it **ASPIRING**?
- Is it **REACHABLE**?
- Is it **TIME**-bound?

Write out an example of a SMART Objective below:

_____

_____

_____

_____

_____

Gospel Life Plan as an Objective

At the first session, give the instructions for the disciple developing their Gospel Life Plan. See previous chapter on this topic. This is to be done by the disciple after session one and completed at a date when you both agree is acceptable. If the GLP is not done within four sessions, it hinders the ability to coach them effectively. It is best to schedule a session when you could talk about the results of their GLP Day. I would suggest the second or third session.

I easily created a table within Evernote where the disciple could record their GLP. The advantage is that they have it in the coaching Notebook where their other sessions exist. Evernote allows the table to expand according to its content, so it is able to be as detailed as a person wants it to be. Below is an example of what it looks like with minimal content.

	Personal	Spiritual	Missional
Call	Shepherd wife	Spiritual Disciplines	Equip & Encourage Pastors and Families
Goals	Daily Significant Encouragement	Prayer Bible Read on Disciplines	Coach Pastors Train in GC
Action	Write letter weekly Weekly date Daily text Trips to see Jack	6 books on Disciplines LIFE Reading Journal Daily	Write Workbook 10 training events in 2014 Call daily Develop Family Coaching
Steward	Plan & Schedule Date night Money for trips to Dad	P & B in morning Read in evening	Calendar!

S – Strategies

The fourth letter in C.R.O.S.S. is *"Strategies."* This is where you will spend the majority of the coaching session. I suggest reserving 30 minutes for men and 40 minutes for women for this section.

When a person goes into a physician's office, the doctor normally interacts with the patient relationally (Connect) and then transitions to inquire about their chief complaint (Objective). The doctor will ask about their past medical treatments and their follow through with therapy or prescription (Review). Once the physician gats that data, they are ready to explore treatment of the patient's chief complaint. This is similar to this phase that we call strategy.

An athletic coach goes through a similar process with their players and team. They need a strategy that is applicable to gain victory over a specific opponent. I coached basketball for 20 years. Our high school team won the conference championship and we had to play in a district tournament whereby the winner advanced to the State Tournament. I watched a video of our opponent late into the evening with my son. At midnight, I crawled into bed and whispered to my wife, "We're going to state." She asked how I knew and I told her that I knew the exact strategy necessary to beat our opponent. At practice on Monday I declared our objective to the team—to beat them by 10 points—and I spent the rest of the week working on the strategy to carry out the objective. After the game, the opposing coach told me that he had not seen a team play them with such patience and focus. We won 44-40.

It is helpful for me to see the coaching as a journey. We have connected in the parking lot and have covenanted to take this journey together. We

have reviewed where we are and have agreed on the objective. As we head toward the objective, we must navigate our way by identifying the well-paved roads, the obstacles, the resources needed, and the people who we will need to achieve the objective.

When I first started coaching, I used to physically draw this picture and I would write the objective in the sign. Then I would envision what it took to get there and I would ask a series of questions.

STRATEGY Questions:

- What resources do you now have that will help facilitate this objective?
- What resources do you need?
- What obstacles stand in the way? Press for all of them.
- What is the first obstacle?
- What people could help you reach this objective?
- How will you address the first obstacle?

I coached a pastor who told me that his objective for the coaching session was to start five new gospel communities. I asked these questions and his answers are in parentheses below.

- How many gospel communities do you have now? (None).
- How many people do you have ready to lead one? (Maybe two).
- What training do you have in place to prepare the leaders? (None. I had not thought about training them).
- What does your church think about implementing this new ministry of gospel communities? (They are not aware of it).
- What does your leadership think about it? (I have not talked with them about it).
- Do you think we should talk about how to start five new gospel communities or how to cast vision to your elders about this? (I hate you). He was kidding...I think.

What other questions could you ask toward strategy?

_____
_____
_____
_____

Brainstorming for Strategy

I have found brainstorming to be a useful tool in coaching when a disciple is stuck. A consultant might just give the disciple the answer, but coaching is helping another person to figure out how to lead self and others. It is similar to giving a man a fish to eat one meal versus teaching a man how to fish. Brainstorming is teaching a person how to think, how to be creative, and how to solve issues with a friend.

I brainstormed with a European network leader how he could raise funds that would free him up to do ministry full-time. I had been in his home and had coached him for a few years. I saw how frugal he lived and how that he had boarders in his home, not necessarily to be hospitable, but to pay the monthly bills. I asked him a powerful question, "What would it mean to you to be freed to develop leaders, start churches, write material, and have enough support to make decisions that did not teeter on finances?" He paused for about 60 seconds. I didn't say a word. I could sense the wheels turning. He then asked sheepishly, "Is that possible?" We proceeded to brainstorm ideas and within three months, he had raised enough money to be fully supported without the need for multiple boarders.

PRACTICE BRAINSTORMING. Come up with as many ways that you can think to free up time to coach four people.

_____
_____
_____
_____
_____

After the strategy section is completed, be sure and take the time to capture any steps of action that could be moved to the Accountability file or write them out clearly in the session notes.

S – Supplication & Spirit

The fifth letter in C.R.O.S.S. is "*Supplication* and *Spirit*." Continual prayer and Holy Spirit-empowerment are key elements to coaching. First, prayer by the coach for the disciple is necessary. The Apostle Paul said he prayed night and day for Timothy (2 Tim 1:3). Second, prayer before the session is needed to ask the Spirit to anoint the time. Third, prayer during the session can take place at any moment. A coach can stop at any point and pray for the disciple. There are no rules that praying at the beginning and end are the only prayers allowed. Fourth, ask how you can pray for the person. This is also a clue what is most important to them at the time. Finally, ask the disciple to close the session in prayer and listen carefully. This is simple, but for some people, it may be the most prayer they have experienced with another person in a long time. People simply do not pray with and for one another like the Bible instructs.

Pray *with* the other person. Don't just pray *for* them, and certainly, don't pray *at* them. This is passive aggressive praying! Pray *with* them. You are in this journey together.

Supplication

- Pray for the disciple regularly.
- Pray before the session for leading.
- Pray during the session whenever led.
- Ask how to pray for them.
- Pray and listen.
- Pray *with* the disciple.

Spirit

The Holy Spirit unites us as believers to Jesus Christ and to His body. The Spirit reveals Christ to us, gives us His life, and makes Christ alive in us. Unfortunately, some movements have become known for their excesses in regard to the Holy Spirit's work and in response, some have neglected the Holy Spirit's continual work in the church, in believers, and in coaching relationships.

You cannot coach effectively without the Holy Spirit. Look over the list below, compiled by Frank Viola.[55] Make a mark by all that are applicable to coaching:

1. He convicts the world of sin, righteousness, and judgment (John 16:8).
2. He guides us into all truth (John 16:13).
3. He regenerates us (John 3:5-8; Titus 3:5).
4. He glorifies and testifies of Christ (John 15:26; 16:14).
5. He reveals Christ to us and in us (John 16:14-15).
6. He leads us (Rom. 8:14; Gal. 5:18; Matt. 4:1; Luke 4:1).
7. He sanctifies us (2 Thess. 2:13; 1 Pet. 1:2; Rom. 5:16).
8. He empowers us (Luke 4:14; 24:49; Rom. 15:19; Acts 1:8).
9. He fills us (Eph. 5:18; Acts 2:4; 4:8, 31; 9:17).
10. He teaches us to pray (Rom. 8:26-27; Jude 1:20).
11. He bears witness in us that we are children of God (Rom. 8:16).

12. He produces in us the fruit or evidence of His work and presence (Gal. 5:22-23).
13. He distributes spiritual gifts and manifestations (the outshining) of His presence to and through the body (1 Cor. 12:4, 8-10; Heb. 2:4).
14. He anoints us for ministry (Luke 4:18; Acts 10:38).
15. He washes and renews us (Titus 3:5).
16. He brings unity and oneness to the body (Eph. 4:3; 2:14-18). A sure evidence of the Holy Spirit working in a group is Love and Unity. Not signs and wonders (those are seasonal and can be counterfeited).
17. He is our guarantee and deposit of the future resurrection (2 Cor. 1:22; 2 Cor. 5:5).
18. He seals us unto the day of redemption (Eph. 1:13; 4:30).
19. He sets us free from the law of sin and death (Rom. 8:2).
20. He quickens our mortal bodies (Rom. 8:11).
21. He reveals the deep things of God to us (1 Cor. 2:10).
22. He reveals what has been given to us from God (1 Cor. 2:12).
23. He dwells in us (Rom. 8:9; 1 Cor. 3:16; 2 Tim. 1:14; John 14:17).
24. He speaks to, in, and through us (1 Cor. 12:3; 1 Tim. 4:1; Rev. 2:11; Heb. 3:7; Matt. 10:20; Acts 2:4; 8:29; 10:19; 11:12, 28; 13:2; 16:6,7; 21:4,11).
25. He is the agent by which we are baptized into the body of Christ (1 Cor. 12:13).
26. He brings liberty (2 Cor. 3:17).
27. He transforms us into the image of Christ (2 Cor. 3:18).
28. He cries in our hearts, "Abba, Father" (Gal. 4:6).
29. He enables us to wait (Gal. 5:5).
30. He supplies us with Christ (Phil. 1:19, KJV).
31. He grants everlasting life (Gal. 6:8).
32. He gives us access to God the Father (Eph. 2:18).
33. He makes us (corporately) God's habitation (Eph. 2:22).
34. He reveals the mystery of God to us (Eph. 3:5).
35. He strengthens our spirits (Eph. 3:16).
36. He enables us to obey the truth (1 Pet. 1:22).
37. He enables us to know that Jesus abides in us (1 John 3:24; 4:13).
38. He confesses that Jesus came in the flesh (1 John 4:2).
39. He says "Come, Lord Jesus" along with the bride (Rev. 22:17).
40. He dispenses God's love into our hearts (Rom. 5:5).
41. He bears witness to the truth in our conscience (Rom. 9:1).
42. He teaches us (1 Cor. 2:13; John 14:26).
43. He gives us joy (1 Thess. 1:6).
44. He enables some to preach the gospel (1 Pet. 1:12).
45. He moves us (2 Pet. 1:21).

46. He knows the things of God (1 Cor. 2:11).
47. He casts out demons (Matt. 12:28).
48. He brings things to our remembrance (John 14:26).
49. He comforts us (Acts 9:31).
50. He makes some overseers in the church and sends some out to the work of church planting [through the body] (Acts 20:28; 13:2).

Coach with the C.R.O.S.S.

C.R.O.S.S. creates a structure for a coach to have an intentional gospel conversation with focused discussions about a disciple's personal, spiritual, and missional life. It is the structure that can lead to gospel transformation. It is a journey together. Coaching is not handing another person a map. Coaching is offering another person your hand to journey through the winding path as they pursue God's calling for their life. God never intended for us to attempt this journey alone. Coaching provides a way to develop leaders, make disciples, and strengthen the feeble hands and weak knees of church leaders (Isa. 35:3; Heb. 12:12).

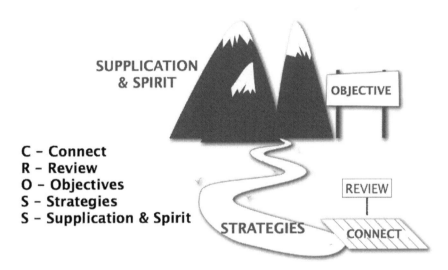

SUPPLICATION & SPIRIT

OBJECTIVE

C – Connect
R – Review
O – Objectives
S – Strategies
S – Supplication & Spirit

REVIEW

STRATEGIES

CONNECT

First Four Coaching Sessions

The first four coaching session samples are found in Appendix 6 to get you started. You will get the hang of it after your first four sessions. These are samples only, templates for you to ask your own questions. You can borrow those that are provided, but every coaching session is different and each subsequent session builds on the one prior. Remember to have fun. This is a journey together with a friend.

11 PRACTICE COACHING

Formal training to make leaders is ineffective. A lot of training focuses on technique, on content, and on curriculum. You absorbed a lot of information throughout this study, but I intentionally integrated visual illustrations for those who learn best in this way. I also integrated kinesthetic learning by encouraging you to write some things down. Finally, I utilized experiential learning to reinforce the skill development. You were asked to engage in multiple conversations to help process the content. My goal was that you would become equipped to competently coach a disciple in the power of the gospel. Gospel Coach Training is more than training, it is skill development. Forbes Magazine contributor Mike Myatt said the following:

> "The solution to the leadership training problem is to scrap it in favor of development. Don't train leaders, coach them, mentor them, disciple them, and develop them, but please don't attempt to train them. Where training attempts to standardize by blending to a norm and acclimating to the status quo, development strives to call out the unique and differentiate by shattering the status quo. Training is something leaders dread and will try and avoid, whereas they will embrace and look forward to development. Development is nuanced, contextual, collaborative, fluid, and above all else, actionable."[56]

Learning Groups or Communities of Practice are effective development opportunities for leaders. *Communities of practice* are a small "group of people informally bound together by shared expertise and passion for a joint enterprise."[57] That is what we want to do at this time. This is the practicum section. It is an important aspect of the learning. Do not skip it—even if it is awkward for you. Some will be uncomfortable, but all who participate will be richer for the experience.

Practice Coaching in Community

It works best to put yourself in groups of three for this community of practice. This triad will spend 60 to 90 minutes together honing skills for coaching. Here is how it is broken down:

1. Person #1 coaches person #2 for 20 minutes while person #3 observes and takes notes. After 20 minutes, person #3 shares observational thoughts about the coach's coaching skill. These are to be helpful observations to make them a better coach. Person #2 can also give feedback to the coach. This takes about 5-10 minutes.

2. Person #2 coaches person #3 for 20 minutes while person #1 observes and takes notes, followed by a 5-10 minute feedback.

3. Person #3 coaches person #1 for 20 minutes while person #2 observes and takes notes, followed by a 5-10 minute feedback.

Coach with the C.R.O.S.S.

Practice all aspects of C.R.O.S.S. coaching in the short time that you have. Truncate the time to fit into 20 minutes.

- **Connect** for 30 seconds.
- **Review** for 1 minute. Ask, "What one or two things could you change in your life that would make a difference?"
- **Objective** for 1 minute. Refine one objective from the question above.
- **Strategies** for 15 minutes. Be sure and identify some specific action items.
- **Supplication & Spirit** for 2.5 minutes. Pray for the disciple and ask the Spirit to empower to follow through.

Notes while Coaching:

_____

_____

_____

_____

_____

_____

_____

_____

_____

_____

_____

Observations on another's coaching:

_____
_____
_____
_____
_____
_____
_____
_____
_____
_____
_____

Feedback on my coaching:

_____
_____
_____
_____
_____
_____
_____
_____
_____
_____
_____

Gospel Coach Certification
Gospel Coach offers certification for those who are interested.

Certification requires seven steps:
1. Read *Gospel Coach: Shepherding Leaders to Glorify God.*
2. Attend a Gospel Coach training event.
3. Take an online test over the book contents and workbook.
4. Choose two disciple-leaders to coach for five sessions each.
5. Demonstrate coaching competence measured by two disciples and a self-evaluation measured through an online assessment.
6. Submit online certification analysis portfolio.
7. Certification.

Appendix 1

WHY EVERY CHURCH LEADER NEEDS A COACH

Every church leader should have a coach to address his personal, spiritual and missional life. Below are thirty reasons that pastors gave to me in my Gospel Coach training:

1. Coaching helps to remind a leader of the Gospel
2. Coaching exposes a leader's blind spots
3. All leaders are capable of succumbing to sin's deception
4. Leaders are models for faithful obedience
5. Coaching is preventative maintenance for a leader
6. The stakes for a church leader are high
7. Coaching models biblical community
8. Coaching provides a prayer partner for the leader
9. Leaders can be prideful
10. Leaders are often lonely
11. Coaching is a practical means for a leader to pay careful attention to self
12. Coaching brings encouragement to the leader
13. Coaching can protect the flock from a leader's mistakes and bad decisions
14. Coaching improves a leader's perspective and objectivity
15. Coaching facilitates the leader's growth and equipping
16. Coaching sharpens a leader's calling
17. Leaders lead where they have walked themselves
18. Coaching is a means for intentional accountability and submission
19. Coaching helps a leader identify and fight arrogance
20. Ministry is a difficult and complicated task
21. Leaders in a coaching relationship model discipleship
22. Shepherds need shepherded
23. Coaching sharpens a leader's skills and abilities
24. Coaching provides a safe sounding board
25. Coaching is fun
26. Coaching encourages friendship
27. Coaching provides affirmation for a leader's decisions
28. Coaching enables personal sanctification
29. Coaching protects family and marital health
30. Coaching is a means to obtain advice from a fellow leader

ABOUT THE AUTHOR

Scott Thomas is a pastor to pastors and their families. Scott served as a pastor in the local church for 32 years, including as a lead pastor for 16 years, a youth pastor for 9 years, and then as an International church-planting network director that God empowered to start over 400 churches. Scott created the Gospel Coach Training and Certification system and is the published author of books to help pastors to develop leaders within the local church. Scott and Jeannie have been married for almost 33 years and have two grown sons, a daughter-in-law, and a granddaughter expected in June (many, many pictures forthcoming).

Scott can be contacted for speaking, training, consulting, and coaching at gospelcoach@gmail.com.

---

[1] Scott Thomas & Tom Wood, *Gospel Coach: Shepherding Leaders to Glorify God* © 2012 (Grand Rapids, MI: Zondervan), loc. 1506.

[2] The main emphasis in Acts 20:28 is to care for the church of God. The Greek word (poimaino) is the same word translated as "shepherd," "care," "rule," and "tend."

[3] Jesus is the chief shepherd. Titus established elders in every church as the undershepherds of Jesus, who is the head of the church. The elders cannot shepherd all of the flock that is among them (1 Peter 5) without deploying and appointing shepherds (pastoral care-givers) under them—under-undershepherds. They are appointed by and through the local church. Just as Paul and Barnabas were sent ONLY after the church confirmed the Holy Spirit's call of them (Acts 13), so the church, through the undershepherd elders, are to entrust certain people to care for others. Shepherding is not a position, neither is pastoring. Elder is a biblical position in the church; caring for the church is the responsibility of all leaders who have been appointed by the elders.

[4] Pay careful attention to self and Pay careful attention to all the flock

[5] http://www.ccel.org/ccel/calvin/calcom37.viii.v.html

[6] Nicoll, W Robertson, Editor: Expositors Greek Testament: 5 Volumes. Out of print.

[7] Scott Thomas & Tom Wood, *Gospel Coach: Shepherding Leaders to Glorify God* © 2012 (Grand Rapids, MI: Zondervan), loc. 163.

[8] The 72 returned to Jesus (vv. 17-24) where He debriefed them, encouraged them, and gave them greater vision for the Kingdom. They had to focus on mission as He put the disciples in a situation that was beyond their abilities. They had to rely on one another in small communities of two. They came back with more questions from their experiences.

[9] Coach Paul had a personal relationship with Jesus (v 1). He had a relationship with his disciple (v. 2). Paul expressed a commitment to the disciple (v. 3). Paul encouraged Timothy personally (v. 4), spiritually (v. 5), and missionally (vv. 6-7). Characteristics of their relationship included knowledge of each other, prayer, trust, fatherhood, challenger, purposeful, and encourager.

[10] Midwestern Theological Seminary is aggressively opening church-based seminaries across multiple locations. Porterbrook is a non-accredited method of church-based training.

[11] Scott Thomas & Tom Wood, Gospel Coach: Shepherding Leaders to Glorify God © 2012 (Grand Rapids, MI: Zondervan), loc. 470.

[12] See Gospel Coach, chapter 2

[13] Tim Chester, *Closing the Window: Steps to Living Porn Free.* (Downers Grove, IL: InterVarsity Press), 2010, loc. 530.

[14] David Powlison, "Idols of the Heart and 'Vanity Fair,'" *Journal of Biblical Counseling*, 13, no. 2 (Winter 1995): 35.

[15] See illustration, Figure 5. From worship, a sense of calling and a generous sacrifice of our own life motivates mission and community. From identity, faith-filled courage and loving leadership empowers mission and community.

[16] Drew Nathan Dyck, *Yawning at Tigers*, (Nashville, TN: Nelson Books), 2014, 54.

[17] *More* is not the problem. *Motivation* is the problem. When leaders are horizontally

driven by ministry results, instead of ministry source—Jesus Christ—the leader begins to wobble spiritually.

[18] Tim Keller, *The Freedom of Self-Forgetfulness*. (Chorley, England: 10Publishing), 2012, loc. 335

[19] http://www.lifewayresearch.com/2010/01/05/pastors-long-work-hours-come-at-expense-of-people-ministry

[20] http://www.britannica.com/EBchecked/topic/403456/narcissism

[21] http://www.britannica.com/EBchecked/topic/403458/Narcissus

[22] Our culture demands that all leaders produce. Sometimes leaders get lost in the potential for ministry and their big vision to reach out to others. Sometimes we work hard because we love Jesus. We just need to learn how to rest and to not be motivated by our performance to validate our standing with God or anyone else. The danger is when leaders believe they earn more favor with God by making more disciples. The baby boomer generation may be the most guilty of this.

[23] http://sbcvoices.com/the-dangers-of-entrepreneurship-in-pastoral-ministry/#sthash.RPbwpkU8.dpuf

[24] See chapter 4 of *Gospel Coach* for a fuller explanation of idols.

[25] Tripp, Paul D. 2012. Dangerous Calling, p. 98.

[26] Roger Pochek, 2007. FAMILY MATTERS AND CHURCH PLANTING

[27] http://enrichmentjournal.ag.org/200603/200603_020_burnout.cfm

[28] Tripp, Paul D. 2012. Dangerous Calling, p. 105.

[29] Matthew Sleeth. 2102. *24/6: A Prescription for a Healthier, Happier Life.* (Tyndale).

[30] http://enrichmentjournal.ag.org/200603/200603_020_burnout_sb_manag.cfm

[31] http://www.bodybuilding.com/fun/behar2.htm

[32] Sleeth, 2012.

[33] Asking "What would it look like?" is a good coaching question to implement. Ask the disciple to envision for themselves what a change in motivation, behavior, or practice would produce for their life.

[34] http://ministrytodaymag.com/index.php/ministry-outreach/service/830-the-significance-of-serving

[35] http://thomrainer.com/2013/09/07/the-lonely-pastor-nine-observations/

[36] C.S. Lewis, *Four Loves*. (Orlando, FL: Harcourt Books, 1988), p. 121.

[37] C.S. Lewis, *Four Loves* (Orlando, FL: Harcourt Books, 1988), p. 89.

[38] Vaughan Roberts, _True Friendship: Walking Shoulder to Shoulder. (Leyland England: 10Publishing, 2013), loc. 66.

[39] Scott Thomas & Tom Wood, *Gospel Coach: Shepherding Leaders to Glorify God* © 2012 (Grand Rapids, MI: Zondervan), p. 35.

[40] See Appendix 1 – Why Every Church Leader Needs a Coach

[41] See chapter 5 of *Gospel Coach* for an explanation of the three aspects for examining life.

[42] Good questions are not complex questions; they are simple questions that get to the heart of the matter quickly.

[43] Rogers, Carl R., and Richard E. Farson. "Active Listening." [1957]. In *Communication in Business Today*. Ed. R. G. Newman, M. A. Danziger, and M. Cohen. Washington, D.C.: Heath and Company, 1987

[44] J. Brownell, Exploring the strategic ground for listening and organizational

effectiveness. *Scandinavian Journal of Hospitality and Tourism, 8*(3), (2008) 211-229.

[45]Judi Brownell, *Listening: Attitudes, Principles, ana Skills.* (Boston: Pearson Education, Inc., 2005).

[46]Floyd, Kory. *Interpersonai Communication.* New York, NY: McGraw-Hill Humanities/Social Sciences/Languages, 2009.

[47] http://www.ctlibrary.com/le/2006/spring/stateofart.html

[48]http://www.gty.org/resources/questions/QA126/what-is-the-pastors-responsibility-besides-preaching-and-studying

[49] Indirect confrontation is when the coach utilizes questions, stories, encouragement, and quotes the disciple's own words (e.g., "victim"). Indirect confrontation emphasizes "we are in this together."

[50] See chapter 11 of *Gospel Coach.*

[51]http://blog.heartpointsapp.com/post/60958151681/breakthrough-christian-goals-setting

[52] See Chapter 12 of *Gospel Coach.* Five Practical Phases of the Coaching Session.

[53] http://www.123test.com/disc-personality-test/

[54] https://www.discinsights.com/whatisdisc#.UxXsCWRdUhV

[55] 50 Things the Holy Spirit Does. http://frankviola.org/2010/11/18/50-things-the-holy-spirit-does/

[56] http://www.forbes.com/sites/mikemyatt/2012/12/19/the-1-reason-leadership-development-fails/

[57] Bogenrieder, I. and Nooteboom, B. Learning Groups: What Types are there? A Theoretical Analysis and an Empirical Study in a Consultancy Firm. Organization Studies February 2004 25: 287-313, doi:10.1177/0170840604040045

Made in the USA
Lexington, KY
11 November 2014